THE APPROACH TO SELF-GOVERNMENT

THE APPROACH TO SELF-GOVERNMENT

BY

SIR IVOR JENNINGS
K.B.E., Q.C., LITT.D., LL.D., F.B.A.
Master of Trinity Hall and Hon. Fellow of St Catharine's College, Cambridge

CAMBRIDGE
AT THE UNIVERSITY PRESS
1958

CAMBRIDGE UNIVERSITY PRESS
Cambridge, New York, Melbourne, Madrid, Cape Town,
Singapore, São Paulo, Delhi, Tokyo, Mexico City

Cambridge University Press
The Edinburgh Building, Cambridge CB2 8RU, UK

Published in the United States of America by
Cambridge University Press, New York

www.cambridge.org
Information on this title: www.cambridge.org/9780521241915

First published 1956
Reprinted 1958
First paperback edition 2011

A catalogue record for this publication is available from the British Library

ISBN 978-0-521-24191-5 Paperback

CONTENTS

PREFACE

TOWARDS the end of 1954 the British Broadcasting Corporation suggested that a series of talks, seeking to apply the experience of the Asian countries of the Commonwealth to the general problem of converting dependent territories into independent countries, would arouse interest in the United Kingdom, and asked me if I would prepare such talks for recording in Karachi or Colombo. I was unable to record the talks until I returned to England in the summer of 1955. Meanwhile I had prepared a script; but the material was so considerable that on my arrival in England I found it necessary to prepare a shorter script, which was broadcast and published in the *Listener*. The interest aroused seemed to justify the publication of the longer script; but in June 1955 I was recalled to Karachi and accordingly was unable to undertake the revision of the script until October 1955. In the text published in this book some of the arguments have been elaborated and some further illustrations inserted. The book nevertheless remains a script prepared for broadcasting, and therefore retains the personal and to some extent autobiographical form appropriate to that medium.

In a preliminary talk recorded in Karachi, and in the first talk of the series, I did my best to emphasise that (apart from a short experience as member of a panel of jurists advising the Commissioner for Eritrea, in East Africa) my experience was limited to Asia. Indeed, though I have had to perform official duties in Singapore, Malaya and Hong Kong, they related to educational and not to constitutional problems. I believe strongly in the importance of local knowledge and experience, and I do not possess that experience so far as the African and Caribbean colonies are concerned. In the main I have relied upon my own experience in advising on constitutional problems in Ceylon, Pakistan and the Maldive Islands, and in seeking to draw lessons from the experience of India. My generalisations may help to suggest ideas in the dependent territories which are now approaching self-government, but I cannot guarantee that they are applicable.

W. Ivor Jennings

Trinity Hall
Cambridge

27 October 1955

I

THE PROBLEM

SOME years ago four jurists were seated in a room in the Palace of the Nations in Geneva. They had been summoned from four different countries by the United Nations Commissioner for Eritrea. Eritrea was a former Italian colony whose disposition had fallen to the General Assembly of the United Nations, and the Assembly had decided that it should become a democratic State, federally united with Ethiopia under the Ethiopian Crown. The task of the jurists was to frame a Constitution in accordance with this decision, so that it could be submitted by the Commissioner to the Constituent Assembly of Eritrea.

It happened that only one of the four jurists had ever been to Eritrea. As they went down to lunch, the Englishman remarked to the Swiss that there was a precedent for framing a Constitution for a country which they had never visited. Jeremy Bentham had sat in Westminster working out constitutional principles for countries almost as far apart as China and Peru. The Swiss jurist replied that there was an even better precedent. Sitting in Geneva, Jean-Jacques Rousseau had drafted a constitution for Poland, a country which he had never visited.

Bentham's theory was that there were fundamental principles, which enabled him or anybody else to work out a constitutional scheme for any country provided that he was given information about its social, political and economic conditions. Nowadays such information is never lacking. All over the world people are making surveys, collecting statistics, writing reports. These documents are always useful and indeed essential, but they rarely tell the constitutional draftsman all that he needs to know. Every Constitution has to be a product of history, even when it comes straight from the draftsman's pen; it is a product of the manner which the country concerned emerged as an independent State, of the conflicts which preceded that emergence and of the forces that have played upon it. The result is sometimes called the genius of the people, but that word must be understood in its etymological sense: it does not imply that the people has some special capacity for government. What it does mean is that every people is unique, and accordingly that every country must have a Constitution to suit itself, a Constitution made to measure, not one bought off the rack.

We in Britain are very familiar with the idea because we have no written Constitution at all, but a mass of laws and institutions which determine our form of government, and this form has evolved over centuries. There are in it relics of feudal monarchy; it has been profoundly influenced by Christianity in general and the Roman Catholic and Protestant churches in particular; much of it reminds us of acute political conflicts which this nation has suffered, including a civil war; it owes something to the Normans, the Danes, the Welsh, the Scots and the Irish as well as to the English. It is, in short, impregnated with our history. If Britain wanted a written Constitution we could not imagine a Mexican or a Pole, or even a Swiss or a Frenchman, drafting it for us unless he had lived among us and had absorbed something of our traditions. Indeed, they are more than traditions, for they create emotions which even one who has lived among us for a long time is unlikely to share.

Our free institutions are the product of a long history,

a gradual development from feudalism to landlordism and from landlordism to modern democracy. Our political writers have rationalised the process, have defended each step and justified each innovation. Their books have influenced thought throughout the Commonwealth and far beyond. The nationalism which develops in a colonial territory is partly a product of individual experience; but it also consists, in very large measure, of a complex of ideas derived from our own history and literature. The combination produces nationalist emotion; and it tends to become not the tempered patriotism which is evident in Britain, but the virulent and aggressive nationalism with which British administrators have to deal in the last stages of colonial development.

The process is so rapid that the whole cycle occupies less than a century. Let us consider the example of India. It must be emphasised at the outset that the nationalism which now prevails in India is an important element in its political cohesion. Socially and economically India is far from being a homogeneous country. Socially it is divided into a confused mass of groups based on language, culture, religion and caste. Economically it consists mainly of millions of peasants living on subsistence agriculture for whom political movements have little if any importance. What keeps India together is the nationalism produced by British rule. It has its unpleasant side; it sometimes causes Indian speakers to misrepresent British policy elsewhere in the Commonwealth because for a generation or more nationalist propaganda has exaggerated and distorted British policy in India; it tends to be aggressive, as we have seen in Hyderabad, Junagarh, Kashmir and Goa; it causes trepidation in Pakistan and Ceylon, because India is potentially a dangerous neighbour so long as nationalism is capable of being converted into chauvinism; but, on the whole, it is the cement which binds India together.

It is, however, a very modern phenomenon. Reading history backwards, politicians of the Indian National Congress regard what we call the Indian Mutiny of 1857 as the first manifestation of Indian nationalism, though that military revolt had no nationalist ideology. The year 1857 is significant in the history of India not because of the Mutiny but because in that year the universities of Bombay, Calcutta and Madras were founded. It added to a thin stream of Indians educated in British universities a broad stream of Indians educated through the medium of the English language but in their own country. It brought western ideas in general and western political ideas in particular to a substantial section of the people of India and created the movement of opinion which became in the next generation the nationalist movement. It completed a scheme of educational establishments, which was gradually broadened, using the medium of the English language. Indians now condemn this use of a foreign language, and regard Lord Macaulay, who advocated the development with his customary exaggeration, as an enemy of the Indian people. It was, however, this infusion of 'English education' which enabled the nationalist movement to be established and gave India sovereign independence within a century. It may be that a more enlightened Government would have developed education through the local languages *pari passu* with education through English: that is still a matter of some controversy. What is plain is that the whole nationalist movement is a product of English education, of the infusion of ideas which access to English literature made possible. The nationalism which, in its extreme form, spurns the West is itself purely western; and it may be that India, which by reason of its size and social structure is a very conservative country, will be the last exponent of nationalist ideas, which are no doubt temporary phenomena like most ideas. The present Indian leaders are all English-educated. If they succeed in maintaining the coherence of India while developing Hindi as the national language and the other Indian languages as provincial languages—and we all hope they will—they will have performed a very remarkable feat; but the feat would have been impossible had the wealthier classes not been educated through English and so provided India with a common political philosophy upon which the nationalist movement was founded.

The first signs of that movement appeared after one generation, but two generations were needed to make it a political force. Its power developed rapidly in the third generation and led to the long conflict of the 'twenties and the 'thirties of this century. It was complicated by the growing antagonism between the Indian National Congress, which was predominantly Hindu, and the Muslim League. Both were nationalist, but whereas the Congress assumed that India was one nation, the League assumed that there were two nations. This conflict led eventually to the establishment of Pakistan, but it also had two other consequences. First, the difficulty of reaching a solution acceptable to all parties led to considerable delay in the attainment of self-government and therefore to increasing virulence in the campaign. Secondly, the sense of frustration created by the conflict caused both parties to 'blame the British' even more than they would have done if there had been no internal conflict. Mahatma Gandhi was not alone in thinking that the problem would solve itself if the 'third party', the British Government, withdrew. What would have happened if the Government of the United Kingdom had 'quit India' without leaving successor authorities we do not know: possibly there would have been civil war, as in Palestine, though Palestine posed a different problem because there the Arabs inside the country were supported by the members of the Arab League, while in India there was a strong army containing both Hindu and Muslim elements. We do know what happened when Britain 'quit India', leaving successor authorities inadequately prepared to maintain law and order. Whole towns and villages were sacked; some sixteen million refugees crossed the new frontier between India and Pakistan; thousands of people were killed, raped or abducted under mob rule. Eight years later there are still refugee camps, organisations for recovering abducted women, and organisations for disposing of refugee property, on both sides of the border.

It is significant, however, that nobody, or hardly anybody, now complains that India and Pakistan were left inadequately organised though, being wise after the event, we may be inclined to think that that will be the verdict of history. There are some, and they are persons of standing and mature judgment, who regret that British rule ever ended: but they are few in number. There are, on the other hand, many in India who regret that the British attempt to hold the balance led to the division of India, and many in Pakistan who regret that the boundaries were so drawn that the Indians were able to seize most of Kashmir without giving the inhabitants the opportunity of deciding upon their future. Such is the strength of nationalist sentiment, however, that the main complaint is that British control lasted so long.

It is not my purpose to pass judgment on these events. Those of us who spent this anxious time in Ceylon did pass judgment and tried to do better in that country, though we recognised that the problem was very much simpler. My point is that this complex of emotions is a factor of the most profound importance in the government of India. Its consequences are to be seen on every page of that enormous document, the Constitution of India. Equally important is the variety of governmental units for which that Constitution has to provide. British rule in India did not attempt to force the whole sub-continent into a uniform framework. On the smaller scale of the United Kingdom we have adapted our institutions to meet new needs as they arose, without seeking to apply any formal theory of government or any concept of the nature of political institutions. Wherever Britain has ruled the same characteristics are noticeable, the same process of adaptation of existing entities. After the independence of India a great process of rationalisation was undertaken by the Congress Government; but the consequences of three centuries of British rule could not be eradicated in three years, and the complications of the Constitution of India are in some measure a consequence of the pragmatic system which the British rulers practised before independence.

In the same way every Constitution must be a product of its environment. Let me give an example from Ceylon. Of the four countries which became independent in 1947—India, Pakistan, Burma and Ceylon—only Ceylon seems likely to retain the monarchy. That decision was quite deliberate. It was to Ceylon's interest to remain in the Commonwealth, and it was the view of Mr D. S. Senanayake, the first Prime Minister, and his colleagues, that if it stayed in the Commonwealth the proper policy was to stay right in. Mr Senanayake was critical of India's decision to try to retain the advantage of membership and at the same time to renounce the formal jurisdiction of the Crown. He thought, and said, that it was not playing the game. In any case, Ceylon might from time to time, and especially in the early years, have to seek assistance from the United Kingdom. It would probably be easier if the application came from one dominion of the Crown to another. There was, however, an even more important argument, though a purely sentimental one. There had been a monarchy in Ceylon for some two thousand or two thousand five hundred years. The ancient Sinhalese kingdoms had been overthrown by the Tamils, but a new kingdom of Kandy had been established, and it had retained its independence even when the maritime provinces were occupied in succession by the Portuguese, the Dutch and the British. By the Kandyan Convention, the sovereignty of the Kandyan provinces was vested in His Britannic Majesty; and the Ceylonese still consider that the Convention is binding on the Queen. Thus, there is a continuous monarchical tradition for over two thousand years, and Mr Senanayake was able to claim that he represented the oldest monarchy in the Commonwealth.

The Crown appears in the Constitution of Ceylon in very much the same form as it appears in the Commonwealth Constitution of Australia. The legal provisions are not quite the same, not only because the Ceylonese politicians were not content to allow the relations between the Crown and its representatives on the one hand, and the Ceylonese Ministers on the other, to be settled by conventions with which the latter were, at the outset, unfamiliar, but also because there is no personal element in the relationship with the monarch. The Queen is Queen of Ceylon, and all possible courtesy and deference was paid to her when she visited the island in

1954: but she is still thought of (incorrectly) as the 'Queen of England', who is also, by the accident of history, Queen of Ceylon. The emotions of the vast crowd, dressed in white banians and brilliantly coloured sarees, squatting and standing in the heat of the morning, under a blue tropical sky, when the Queen opened the Parliament of Ceylon, were necessarily very different from those of the crowd which saw her drive from Westminster to Buckingham Palace at the end of her long, trying but triumphant tour. The monarchy in the Constitution of Ceylon must therefore be different from the monarchy in the British Constitution, or even from that in the Constitution of Australia.

A further example is even more relevant. We cannot imagine the British Constitution working without parties: but the British parties have grown out of the local environment. They have their origins at least as far back as the Civil War; their evolution has been affected by conflicts of religion, economic interest, race and even personality—for our party organisation has depended upon the ideas of thousands of politicians from, let us say, Oliver Cromwell to Ramsay MacDonald. This history has created a complex of emotions helping towards the conflict of parties by which the complexion of Parliament and the Government, their relations with each other and the electorate, are determined. That system cannot be reproduced in a different environment and among a different people; and accordingly one must be wary in adapting the British Constitution in other countries, for a different party system, or perhaps no system at all, will be developed.

Consider, for instance, the country which is at the moment producing a Constitution for itself. Until recently the politics of Pakistan were dominated by the Muslim League, an organization which claimed the support of all the Muslims of undivided India in its demand for Pakistan, and which then claimed the loyalty of all the Muslims of Pakistan because it had enabled the Muslims of India to achieve nationhood. During the eight years which have elapsed since independence, however, it has lost much of its support, especially in East Pakistan. Consequently, though the League dominated the first Constituent Assembly, elected in 1947, it held only a minority of the seats in the second Assembly, elected in 1955. The parties which had virtually superseded it in East Pakistan thought less of the unity of Pakistan than of the autonomy of East Bengal.

As I came away from the first meeting of the new Assembly, in Muree, on one of the foothills of the great Himalayan range, I heard one member say to another that it was very different from the first Assembly. No doubt the legislature which is established under the new Constitution will be different from both: but the point is that all of them will be very different from the Parliament of the United Kingdom. To draft that Constitution on the assumption that the party conflict in the Parliament of Pakistan would be like the party conflict in the Parliament of the United Kingdom would be the height of folly: indeed, much of the discussion about the content of the Constitution has been due to the anticipation that the two-party system of the United Kingdom will not operate, but that there is more likely to be a collection of fluctuating political groups, some of them having purely local or regional objectives. The division of the country into two parts, separated by a thousand miles of Indian territory, together with the composite nature of the people, seems likely to override the unity of Islam which originally conferred a virtual monopoly upon the Muslim League.

Let me give a last example, again from Ceylon.

THE PROBLEM

Twenty years ago I gave lectures in London on the Constitution of that country, which was then in the transitional stage between colonial status and independence. The documents showed that one of the main problems of the transition was the strength of communalism among the Sinhalese and the Tamils, the Buddhists and the Hindus. Though it was not part of my course, I worked out for myself the sort of solution that might be suggested. Ten years later I was employed in Ceylon, and it became my duty to suggest a solution to the Ceylonese Ministers. That solution, which has now been in operation for over seven years, had no connection whatever with the solution which I had worked out in London ten years before. Experience teaches. With all respect to the memory of Jeremy Bentham, one cannot sit in Westminster and draft a Constitution for Mexico unless one knows a good deal more about Mexico than appears in the reference books.

That proposition is a little disturbing. These talks were prepared in Ceylon and Pakistan. Here are two notable examples of dependent territories which have become independent. Moreover, the script flew with me over a country which provides the third and the greatest of the precedents, that of India. The problem now is to develop self-governing institutions in other parts of the Commonwealth—in Malaya, Africa and the West Indies. Will the experience of India, Pakistan and Ceylon have any relevance to the problems in those colonies? Clearly one cannot sit in the Constituent Assembly Building in Murree or Karachi and draft a Constitution for the Gold Coast. There are, however, common elements which make it possible at least to define the problem.

In the first place Britain has been remarkably successful in propagating British constitutional ideas throughout the Commonwealth. Everywhere are to be found village Hampdens, mute inglorious Miltons, Cromwells guiltless of their countries' blood. There are politicians as eloquent as Burke, and in Burke's own language. There are lawyers as tough as 'tough old Coke, the toughest man England ever knew', and as ready to quote Coke's *Institutes* or Blackstone's *Commentaries* or the Law Reports as any young man in the Temple. There are financial experts who know every piece of red tape that was ever tied in Whitehall and who understand why it exists. Some months ago it was suggested to the Drafting Committee of the Constituent Assembly of Pakistan that they insert a clause whose desirability seemed to flow from the experience of the United States of America. At once objections were raised, based on the experience of Britain. As I crossed off the proposal on my agenda I remarked that they were more English than I was, and I thought of the declaration of the barons at Merton in 1236: 'nolumus leges Angliae mutare', we do not want to change the laws of England.

There are reasons for this remarkable success. The freedom and tolerance which flowed from the Civil War, the Restoration, and the Revolution of 1688 have made the Englishman, and the Scot too, a very independent person. Moreover, the British administrator in a colony, whatever his defects may have been, almost invariably had one quality which is still talked about everywhere between Dondra Head and the Khyber Pass, his sense of justice. He could always be trusted to be fair. There is a Sinhalese saying which sounds like a pun when it is translated into English, 'the fairness of the white man'. Now a person in a colony who speaks the language of the English, but who has been treated by them as an inferior because of the colour of his skin or the immaturity of his social and political background, probably will not like the British. He may regard them as the oppressors of his people. He may have spent years in their gaols. Nor does he want to become what in Asia is called a 'brown sahib', a person who apes the mannerisms of the British. Nevertheless he accepts their fundamental constitutional principles. He judges British administrators by their own standards and criticises them if they fall short of them.

Moreover, the self-government which the nationalist politician wants for his own country is the self-government which the British have in their own country. The phrase used is often 'responsible government'. That is a technical term for a system of government like that in Britain, where the Cabinet is responsible to Parliament. There are other forms of self-government, such as that which operates in the United States. Nevertheless, the colonial politician thinks in British terms, and therefore he asks for responsible government. The phrase itself is attractive. It implies responsibility to the representatives of his own people and not to the Secretary of State for the Colonies in Westminster. There is, however, something more in the idea. The fact that responsible government may have a more technical meaning, the system of Cabinet Government which operates in the United Kingdom, is irrelevant, because the British Constitution is undoubtedly successful. The British do know how to govern themselves. Year after year, decade after decade, even century after century for those who read history, the British Constitution goes flowing on like Tennyson's brook. British policy may be objectionable to those who think they have suffered from it; but undoubtedly the machinery of government enables that policy to be carried out.

The war was a fine demonstration of the British Constitution. Mr Neville Chamberlain went out at the moment of danger and Winston Churchill came in. He defied the enemy in tones that rang round the world. In the dark watches of the night the chimes of Big Ben were heard everywhere, often muffled lest the enemy hear them too: and they were followed by the calm, unruffled voice of the B.B.C. announcer. The Mother of Parliaments was standing and the royal standard was flying over Buckingham Palace. The finest demonstration, however, came at the end of the war, when the people of Britain voted Mr Churchill out of office and Mr Attlee simply walked in. The fact that most colonial people did not like Winston Churchill's views on the Colonial Empire added value to the demonstration.

Other Constitutions do not appear to be so successful. Senator McCarthy is the latest of a long line of demagogues to bring discredit upon the Constitution of the United States. The changes of government in France are so frequent that hardly anybody in the Commonwealth overseas can remember the name of the Prime Minister; and, besides, France did not react to Hitler as Britain reacted. The Scandinavian countries and the Netherlands are as successful as Britain, but nobody hears much about them. For the rest, where is a Constitution that can be copied? Spain, Italy, South America, Germany, the countries behind the Iron Curtain, are no precedents except, in the last case, for the communists, who claim not a Constitution but a revolution. Britain, Canada, Australia and New Zealand therefore supply the precedents.

This can be demonstrated by recent experience. The Irish Free State set the example, though it was not a colony. The advisers of the Constituent Dáil collected the Constitutions of the world and published them. Only one Constitution was missing, that of the United Kingdom, for the obvious reason that it was unwritten.

Probably the Provisional Government, whose members had just completed a successful revolution, did not feel that the omission was of any importance. The Constitution enacted in 1921 did in fact contain a number of provisions not taken from Britain. Over the next twelve years, however, those innovations were eliminated by legislation, and the new Republican Constitution of 1937, which is still in force in Ireland, was in all essentials the British Constitution, with a President in place of the Queen.

Ceylon was the first Crown Colony to achieve independence—for Canada, Australia, New Zealand and South Africa were never Crown Colonies—and the Ceylonese Ministers, who prepared the draft in 1943, knew exactly what they wanted. Their terms of reference, the Declaration of 1943, did not permit of the Dominion status which they sought. Nevertheless, the draftsman was instructed to get as near to a Dominion Constitution as—and perhaps a little nearer than—the terms of reference warranted. He kept before him the Constitution of Australia; but, since Australia has a federal Constitution and Ceylon needed a unitary one, he had constantly to appeal from Australia to Britain.

India and Pakistan were provided with Constituent Assemblies, and meanwhile were governed by the Government of India Act, 1935, suitably modified to permit of self-government. The Act was drafted in London, mainly on British precedents, and the amendments brought it nearer the British Constitution. Both Assemblies contained eminent constitutional lawyers trained in the British tradition. Like the Irish, however, they felt no great friendliness towards Britain and they tried to inform themselves about constitutional principles elsewhere. Both Constitutions had to be federal, and therefore founded on the Government of India

Act: but the experience of other federal countries, particularly Canada, Australia, the United States, and the U.S.S.R., was studied. In Pakistan an analysis was made of the solutions provided in various countries to the problems that were before the Constituent Assembly, and reference was made not only to the Constitutions just mentioned, but also to South Africa, India, Ireland, Germany, Yugoslavia and especially the Constitutions of Islamic Republics.

In the end, however, what may be called the British prejudices of the lawyers proved to be dominant. The Constitution of India is based on the Government of India Act and is so full of British constitutional ideas that it may be said to be a series of lessons in British constitutional principles. India is a federal republic, and yet there are responsible Governments of the British type both in New Delhi and in the States. The detailed provisions, especially those relating to the judiciary, are even more redolent of British constitutional experience.

The experience of Pakistan is even more interesting. One of the reasons which enabled the British Constitution, suitably adapted, to work in India is that Indian politics are dominated by the Indian National Congress, a body which enjoys great prestige because it was the party of Mahatma Gandhi and is the party of Jawaharlal Nehru. What is more, it was the party which brought independence to India. During the struggle for that independence many Indian leaders obeyed the decisions of the Congress and suffered severely for their political views. It is a universal trait of human nature that one should feel greater loyalty to an institution for which one has had to make sacrifices than to one which has heaped honours on one's head. In consequence of these factors, and in spite of all the conflicts of personality and power, which have been numerous since 1947, the

Congress still dominates the Union and the great majority of the States. The absence of a strong Opposition is at this stage less relevant, though India may run into difficulties if the Congress either becomes corrupt or breaks up, because there is no Opposition ready to form a Government.

If Pakistan had been able to produce a Constitution as quickly as India, it might have followed the same road. Its leaders had, however, a much more difficult task. It took over only three complete Provinces, Sind, Baluchistan and the North-West Frontier. It also had the larger slice of the Punjab, including the capital city, Lahore. In East Bengal, which contains more than half the population, it did not even have the Provincial capital. Completely new administrations had to be built up in Karachi and Dacca. Even in Peshawar, Lahore, Hyderabad and Quetta, however, large numbers of public employees had been Hindus who migrated to India as soon as partition occurred. The new Central and Provincial administrations had to be built up from a miscellaneous collection of local people and refugees from other parts of the sub-continent. What is more, while these organisations were being established, extensive rioting broke out in many cities and all along the new frontier with India. The police were disorganised and there was no Pakistan army, for the battalions of the pre-partition Indian army had, as a matter of policy, been mixed racially, so that a battalion stationed at, say, Rawalpindi might contain a company of Muslims and companies of Dogras and Sikhs as well.

The first year, therefore, had to be occupied in organisation, and at the end of it Mohammed Ali Jinnah, whose position in the Muslim League was even more powerful than that of Nehru in the Congress, died. There was nobody of his stature left in the League, but

Liaquat Ali Khan kept the machine working until he was assassinated in 1951. Theoretically the Muslim League continued to dominate; but its lack of outstanding personalities, and the conflicts which arose among the lesser men, made it a mere shadow of what it might have been. In the East Bengal election of March 1954 it was practically wiped out and it became plain—even before the League failed to obtain a majority in the second Constituent Assembly elected in June 1955—that Pakistan would follow a different road from India. It would not have two strong parties, as in Britain, nor one strong party with a variety of Opposition groups, as in India, but a handful of competing groups.

In such circumstances I was set the task of producing a suitable Constitution, and by way of experiment I was asked to draft a Constitution in which the American idea of an executive irremovable for four years was grafted on to a British system of representation. It was not intended, as was alleged at the time, to produce an undemocratic system. On the contrary, it was thought that a system in which the nature of the Government was determined by bargains between the leaders of political groups, as in France, was likely to be less democratic and more corrupt than a system in which the Government was given four years to carry out its policy and then compelled to appeal to the people to re-elect it or turn it out. I did my best, but the result was not very satisfactory.

It could not be assumed that the conventions accepted in the United States would be acceptable in Pakistan, and accordingly it was necessary to provide means for solving, for instance, conflicts between the executive and the legislature. The result was thought to be undemocratic, though I do not think it was less democratic than the Constitution of the United States is in practice. I had to admit that the American system could easily be converted into a dictatorship, as it is in most South American States, and that the fusion of British and American ideas was something of an experiment whose success neither I nor anybody else could guarantee. The conclusive argument which led to the rejection of the scheme was, however, that the people of Pakistan were so familiar with the British Constitution that any fundamental departure from it would be regarded with profound suspicion.

There are, however, two exceptions in the Constitution of India which prove the rule. The Constitution contains what are called 'Directive Principles of State Policy'. This idea comes from Eire, which took it from Republican Spain. The origin is instructive, for both countries accept a common philosophy elaborated by the Roman Catholic Church: and this was so in Spain even though the Republic was socialist and anti-clerical. In India the Congress, which had obtained independence, wanted to write its political philosophy into the Constitution. This idea, of putting a formulated political philosophy into a Constitution, may undoubtedly be regarded as un-British. Nevertheless, British constitutional prejudice peeped out. It was realised that, given the British principle of judicial supremacy, which is of course illustrated in the United States even more strongly than in Britain, the effect of putting political philosophy into the Constitution would be to require the courts of law to decide whether legislation did or did not accord with that philosophy. It was therefore specifically provided that that should not happen: the Directive Principles of State Policy were to be fundamental in the governance of the country, but were not to be enforceable in any court. To the sceptical English lawyer, which also means the sceptical Indian lawyer, this means that the Directive Principles are pieces of political propaganda which may safely be ignored.

The second breach with British tradition is the inclusion of a Bill of Rights in the Constitution. That is not so un-British as it appears to be, for it comes from the United States. What the United States tried to do was to put into the Bill of Rights some of the principles of personal and political liberty which had, it was thought, been ignored by the Government of George III. Every phrase of the American Bill of Rights is redolent of British constitutional history. The Indian Bill of Rights is even more British in its texture, for it derives mainly from a book which three generations of Indian law students have had to read before they could pass their examinations, *The Law of the Constitution*, by A. V. Dicey, Vinerian Professor of English Law in the University of Oxford. It incorporates what Dicey called 'the Rule of Law', or what is perhaps better described as 'Liberty according to Law', that nice balance between liberty and law which England established through the conflicts of the seventeenth century and the developments of the eighteenth. In spite of the American Bill of Rights, that liberty is even better protected in Britain than in the United States, and what the Indian lawyers tried to do was to formulate that part of English constitutional law which dealt with personal and political liberty. Pakistan is not so ambitious. It has left more to the common law and to the normal working of political institutions: but that is even more British, for in Britain we have no Bill of Rights; we merely have liberty according to law; and we think—truly, I believe—that we do the job better than any country which has a Bill of Rights or a Declaration of the Rights of Man.

The case I am making is not that all this is right and proper and that a colonial people will be happy if it follows British precedents. What I am saying is that, wherever Britain has ruled, her constitutional ideas prevail, and that our task is eased because we have to adapt those ideas to local conditions. It is a rule of English constitutional law that when a territory becomes one of the dominions of the Crown the local law remains unaltered until it is amended, and the practice is to let it stand. The result is that the Commonwealth contains the most remarkable collection of laws in the world. Roman-Dutch Law, which has long since disappeared in the Netherlands, is in operation in South Africa, Southern Rhodesia and Ceylon; old French Law is administered in Quebec and the French codes in Mauritius; Hindu Law and Muslim Law are in operation in India and Pakistan; ancient Sinhalese Law and Tamil custom are in force in Ceylon; there are relics of Spanish Law in some of the West Indies; and tribal laws operate in many parts of Africa. Nevertheless, British constitutional law operates throughout the Commonwealth and will never be extinguished; it is insidiously permeative. Just as the United States built its law upon Blackstone's *Commentaries*, so the standard works on law and politics become the authoritative works of every country that attains independence within—or, as Burma shows, without—the Commonwealth.

As I have said, this is important. To show how important it is, let us return to the example of the four jurists sitting in Geneva to work out a Constitution for Eritrea. Their task was to formulate a Constitution for a democratic State federally united with Ethiopia. At the moment no question arises about this federal relationship. A democratic State has to be established: how shall it be done? The French lawyer thought in terms of the French Revolution, the Declaration of the Rights of Man, the Sovereignty of the People, and the labours of a host of eminent French jurists for the last 150 years. The English lawyer thought of the monarchy (the Emperor of Ethiopia), the legislature, the franchise, the decisions of courts about fundamental liberties. In other words, the French lawyer thought in terms of juristic principles, while the English lawyer thought in terms of political and legal institutions. They both produced drafts, and they were as alike as chalk and cheese. One clause of the French draft particularly caused discussion. The vote was to be 'unique, equal and secret'. The English lawyer objected: he said that a person might possibly have two votes in different capacities; that it was impossible so to delimit constituencies that all the votes were equal; that in certain circumstances (particularly among the nomadic tribes on the Sudanese border) the vote might not be secret. The French lawyer agreed, but explained that he was merely laying down a principle which would be worked out in detail by organic laws, and they would prescribe exceptions to the general principle. The English lawyer replied that if a general principle was enacted in the Constitution it became a rule of law, and no exceptions could be created to it except under the authority of the Constitution itself, and accordingly if there were to be exceptions they ought to be in the Constitution.

The conflict was never resolved because the panel broke up owing to the other duties of its members. Later a new panel, imbued with the French tradition, was constituted. A Constitution was drafted by a French lawyer, was accepted by the United Nations Commissioner and the Constituent Assembly, and is said to work very well. No doubt it works well because the ideas of French jurists are accepted. It would not work well in the Commonwealth, because some lawyer, bred to the British tradition, would start thinking in terms of injunctions, mandamus, certiorari, prohibition, quo warranto, and above all habeas corpus. An Indian or Pakistani or African judge would not understand general principles which had implicit exceptions. He would say that it was his business to apply 'the law and the law alone'. He would no doubt quote the *Case of Proclamations* and the *Case of Prohibitions*, *Rex* v. *Hampden* and the decision of the Supreme Court of the United States in *Marbury* v. *Madison*. He knows nothing of general principles; his concern is with the law.

That kind of conflict cannot arise in the Commonwealth. Our ways of thought have been adopted by our pupils, and indeed our pupils have begun to give lessons to their teachers. The British constitutional tradition is shared by the United States, but with a difference so substantial that it is the source of a new tradition, which has spread to Central and South America, to the Caribbeans, and even to Japan and the Philippines. It has, too, reacted on the British tradition as exhibited in Canada, Australia, India and Pakistan; but India and Pakistan have also learned from Canada, Australia and South Africa. All these countries, as well as Ireland, Ceylon, the West Indies, the African territories and Malaya, have learned from Britain and from each other and have experimented for themselves. In consequence we have a series of precedents so vast that hardly anyone, and perhaps no one, knows all of them. Nevertheless they are tucked away in one's memory or at least accessible in the books. When a member of a Drafting Committee or Constituent Assembly asks a question about the means to overcome a local difficulty, it is as if he puts a coin in a slot machine. Out pops a precedent; perhaps not exactly in point, but near enough to suggest a line of development.

One soon reaches the conclusion that there is no

constitutional problem that this enlarged British tradition, or perhaps more correctly this Anglo-American tradition, cannot solve. One must beware of such facile assumptions. Certainly the constitutional lawyer would not admit that there is any constitutional problem that he cannot solve by an appropriate draft: but it must be remembered that he solves it only on paper. He creates the legal framework for the establishment of institutions, but the institutions consist of men and women: not only the men and women who rule but also the men and women who are ruled, for in a democratic system there is constant interaction. The Americans say that they have a government not of men but of laws. What they mean is that the powers of their men are limited by the laws; so are ours, and perhaps more so; though with us the laws are more easily changed. They do not mean that the quality of the government of the United States does not depend upon the men who administer the legal powers. The real problem in any country, and not least in a country which is moving towards self-government, is not to draft a Constitution or to make the laws, but to find men and women capable of running the machinery of government.

II

THE PEOPLE

ABRAHAM LINCOLN, in his Gettysburg Speech during the American Civil War, gave the most famous and most apt description of democracy. He expressed the hope 'that this nation, under God, shall have a new birth of freedom, and government of the people, by the people, for the people, shall not perish from the earth'. It is sometimes forgotten that he used 'freedom' and the equivalent of 'democracy' in the same sentence. A so-called 'people's democracy' which allows no freedom is not a democracy and the people do not govern. It reminds me of an argument which I had with a Nazi lawyer after Hitler seized power. After a controversy in public at an unofficial conference, I went up to him in the usual tolerant English way so as to show that our differences were not personal. At the next meeting, when he thought I was not present, he stated that he had met the leader of the British delegation privately and that they had completely agreed. He was right: we had agreed that 'liberty' meant one thing in Britain and another in Germany: what he called 'liberty' I called 'tyranny'.

There is, however, no fear that government by the people will perish from the earth. We in the Commonwealth are busy extending the area of free democracy. In 1920 there were six free democracies in the Commonwealth—the United Kingdom, Canada, Australia, New Zealand, Newfoundland and, if one ignores the Africans, South Africa. Thirty-five years later we have added five more—Ireland, India, Pakistan, Ceylon and

Burma. Leaving out Ireland and Burma, which freely and peacefully left the Commonwealth, and allowing for the fact that Newfoundland is now a Province of Canada, we have in the Commonwealth eight independent democratic nations containing nearly 600 million free people. How many more there will be after another twenty-five years nobody knows, for we do not know what political combinations will be formed. We do know that it is the policy of Her Majesty's Government to raise all the colonial peoples to self-government: and nowadays, I think, it is rarely doubted.

For many years the Indian politicians, basing their opinion on what they thought to be the experience of Ireland—which was a very special case, generally misunderstood—and aided by a good deal of communist propaganda both directly and indirectly, believed that self-government could be obtained only by force (or what proved to be in practice very much the same thing) by non-violent non-co-operation or *satyagraha*. It is reasonably clear that they were mistaken, for in neighbouring Ceylon the opposite view was taken, and Ceylon's independence came only a few months after the enactment of the Indian Independence Act. Nor is it true, as some Indians have alleged, that the Indian 'struggle for freedom' led to the independence of Ceylon. One can never determine exactly how far ideas are moulded by events—in this case the ideas of His Majesty's Government—but in the view of those who were working for the independence of Ceylon the complications of the Indian problem and the behaviour of the Indian politicians were actually retarding development in Ceylon. It is believed that the scheme which Mr D. S. Senanayake put before the British Cabinet in 1945 would have been accepted but for the fact that proposals for India were simultaneously under consideration. Because of the conflict between the Indian Congress and the Muslim League, the Ceylon scheme could not be applied to India, and it was evidently thought undesirable to complicate the Indian problem by solving the easier problem of Ceylon. The result was the postponement of Ceylon's independence by two years, the scheme accepted in 1947 being necessarily less favourable to the United Kingdom than Ceylon had been willing to accept in 1945.

In any case, all doubts should now be set at rest by the attitude of the Colonial Office and its local representatives. It is not always appreciated that what Britain is trying to do is to overcome the local difficulties in the way of 'freedom' or independence. These difficulties, as I hope to make plain, are invariably substantial. Nor are they always appreciated by the local political leaders. It does happen sometimes that British officials exaggerate the difficulties; to ask how political institutions will work in, say, five years' time is to enter the realm of prophecy, and it is very easy to be mistaken. It is, however, as easy to be excessively optimistic as it is to be excessively pessimistic. Usually the local politicians are in the optimistic camp and the officials in the pessimistic camp; but sometimes the officials do not foresee all the difficulties and try to go too fast. In any case the policy cannot now be doubted. Every dependent territory in the Commonwealth is destined to be self-governing, either as a political unit or as part of a larger political unit. This does not necessarily mean that a small and isolated unit like Gibraltar or St Helena can become a sovereign State; but they do not affect the general principle, and in any case these examples are too peculiar to be dealt with in these talks.

The essential condition is that the people should be able to govern themselves. It is here that difficulty arises.

In every colony there are able men and women who are fully capable of bearing the burdens of government. Many of them are graduates of British universities. They know that they are as intelligent and as able as the average British politician or administrator. They take personally the allegation that they are 'not fit to govern'. They know it to be untrue of themselves, and they doubt if we really believe it. They suspect it to be the product of racial or colour prejudice, or perhaps a device for giving jobs to our young men or profits to our capitalists. It is indeed an unfortunate phrase which ought not to be used. It is comparatively easy to find people who are fit to hold the reins: but the problem of government is not a problem of finding people who can become politicians. The machinery is complex and its efficiency depends upon a number of factors which I must examine in turn. One such factor is the character of the people. 'Government by the people' is no fiction. In a democracy the people really do take an active part in government, and the fact that one can find twenty university graduates capable of forming a Cabinet does not imply that the responsibility for governing their country can forthwith be handed over to them. To study this particular aspect of the problem we must return to the United Kingdom, upon whose precedents the whole system of responsible government is based.

The people of the United Kingdom number some fifty million, of whom some thirty-five million, being adult British subjects, have the right to vote. Education has been compulsory for seventy-five years, with the result that every adult citizen, unless he is mentally deficient, can read and write, form an opinion on matters of policy, at least in so far as they affect him personally, and even make some attempt to understand what his political leaders are arguing about. Nearly every household buys at least one newspaper a day, and the circulations of the popular newspapers run into millions. Over twelve million people have licences for wireless sets, so that nearly every household has a set, and there is a complicated network of broadcasting stations sending out programmes all day. To this network is being added a network of television stations, and already four million people watch a popular programme. Thus the United Kingdom has a population nearly every member of which is capable of taking an active interest in political questions. What is more, he does. He may say that he 'is not interested in politics': but (though he does not always realise it) every day he expresses some opinion on some political question, even if he merely remarks that 'it didn't ought to be allowed'. One consequence is that he is capable of taking a decision about the policies of the political parties, even if his reasons would not stand logical analysis. The number of electors voting at a general election is between 75 and 85 per cent of those entitled to vote; and many of those not voting do so deliberately because they disagree with the views of all the candidates.

This population is homogeneous in several ways, which are seldom found in a colony. First, it is relatively homogeneous economically. In a colony there is usually a vast population living at a standard which is now quite unknown in the United Kingdom. The word 'poor' is relative; and there is no family in the United Kingdom which would not be described as 'middle-class' in a colony. Even the word 'rich' is relative; and, though most of our comparatively rich families would be regarded as very rich in most colonies, the spread of incomes in the United Kingdom is much smaller than it is in most dependent territories, because large incomes are heavily reduced by income tax and surtax. This means that class divisions, though evident, are much wider in Asia and Africa than in the United Kingdom, and those class divisions have important political consequences.

Secondly, the people of the United Kingdom are virtually homogeneous in respect of language. Except for a few people in rural Wales and the islands of Scotland, everybody speaks, reads and writes English. The absence of this homogeneity was one of the problems in India, Pakistan and Ceylon. The Indian Constitution lists thirteen modern languages as capable of being official languages in the States, and there is agitation to add to the list. The number of dialects is in the region of 600. Pakistan has two main languages, Urdu and Bengali, but there are several others whose use is widespread. Ceylon has two 'national languages', Sinhalese and Tamil. In all three countries English is the medium of administration and the language generally (but not exclusively) used in the legislatures, but it is spoken by only a fraction of the people. The fact that these countries have attained independence, as well as the experience of countries like Canada, South Africa, Switzerland and Belgium, shows that a single language is not essential; but it needs to be emphasised that the United Kingdom is almost monolingual and that this has important political consequences.

The English, the Welsh, the Scots and the Ulster Irish have different origins and histories and therefore different local loyalties; but those local loyalties are aspects of a common loyalty to the Queen; and, except among a few extremists, they have no political consequences. This is not only unusual but also important. How important it is the people of the United Kingdom themselves know, for they never succeeded in bringing the Southern Irish to the same sense of common endeavour. Nevertheless, the Southern Irish are more closely akin to the peoples of Great Britain than is the case in many parts of the Commonwealth, because the peoples of western Europe share a common tradition founded upon Greek philosophy, Roman law and the Christian religion. There are of course religious differences, as Ireland again demonstrates: but the differences between Roman Catholics and Protestants are small compared with the differences among the other great religions of the world, Islam, Hinduism and Buddhism. These differences have not prevented the independence of India, Pakistan, Ceylon and Burma: but it is significant that British India had to be divided between India and Pakistan, the one predominantly Hindu and the other predominantly Muslim. That division caused hardship to millions and death to hundreds of thousands. Even now there are refugee camps on both sides of the border and the problem of refugee property has not been solved.

It is necessary to stress this homogeneity because the people of the United Kingdom, being used to it, do not appreciate its importance, while educated people in the colonies, anxious for self-government, do not realise that upon it depends in large measure the success of the British system of government. Politically, it has two effects.

In the first place, it enables a party system to be developed on national lines, cutting through all differences of race, religion and locality. Three national parties put forward nearly 98 per cent of the candidates and win over 99 per cent of the votes. Indeed, elections are dominated by the Conservative and Labour parties, which put forward nearly 90 per cent of the candidates and win nearly 97 per cent of the votes. Elections are thus fought on national issues.

Secondly, and perhaps this is even more important, homogeneity makes it possible to speak of a continuing though changing 'public opinion'. Its influence on the process of government is profound. Every politician is aware of it, because his chance of election depends upon his electorate approving the policy of his party. In many immature democracies, including those of India, Pakistan and Ceylon, the success of a candidate depends primarily on his personality and his influence in the locality. He is a candidate in the constituency, not because he advocates a particular policy, but because he is likely to be supported by the electors for reasons peculiar to himself. He belongs to the right community (defined by race, religion, caste or all three); his family has been prominent in the locality for some time, perhaps for generations; he is known for his good works, or perhaps for less worthy reasons; he is likely to be chosen because his personality and his record in these respects are more satisfactory than those of his opponents. What party he belongs to and what policy he advocates are comparatively unimportant. It is not so in the United Kingdom. There the electoral prospects of a candidate depend essentially upon the policy of his party and this means, especially in constituencies in which the parties are equally balanced, upon the popularity or unpopularity of the Government's actions. A slight swing of opinion will put the Government out and the Opposition in. Every Government has to take unpopular decisions, hoping that its popularity will be restored before the next election: but the movements of opinion have to be carefully studied lest unpopularity develop like a snowball. Government by the people is thus a reality in the United Kingdom because in the long run, and often in the short run, public opinion decides.

If self-government in the colonies had to await the

development of a population as homogeneous and as politically mature as that of the United Kingdom it would never happen. The British Constitution has grown up with the British people. In a dependent territory one has to create institutions by legal enactments which will, one hopes, meet the special conditions of the country. Even where the population is much like that of Britain, a transplanted British institution will probably grow in a different manner because the soil is different. It was, for instance, not easy to get Cabinet Government working in the Australian colonies. In the old Province of Canada, which is now the two Provinces of Ontario and Quebec, there was even greater difficulty, mainly because of the conflict between the settlers of English origin and the settlers of French origin. There was a difference of language, a difference of religion and a difference of other traditions. Nobody alleged that either the English or the French were 'unfit for self-government': it was simply that the conflict of tradition made it difficult to establish institutions which would function.

A solution was found eventually. Canada West, now called Ontario, and Canada East, now called Quebec, were converted—or strictly speaking reconverted—into separate Provinces; and to them were added Nova Scotia, New Brunswick and Prince Edward Island so as to form a federation of Provinces under the name of the Dominion of Canada, with a Constitution similar in principle to that of the United Kingdom, as the British North America Act makes plain. The credit must be given not to the constitutional lawyers, though they drafted an instrument which now applies to a Canada containing ten Provinces and so helped to create a great nation. The credit must go to those who took the decisions, and especially to John A. Macdonald of Canada

West and Etienne Cartier of Canada East, who subordinated their local loyalties to the larger patriotism which all Canadians now exhibit.

As a result of the experience of Asia, emphasis upon local, racial, religious, linguistic or other loyalties is now called 'communalism'. No solution of the Canadian problem was possible so long as the English-Canadians and the French-Canadians concentrated on their communal objectives and emotions. A solution was possible when a larger patriotism was created. That larger patriotism did not involve the suppression of communal ideas. On the contrary, Quebec has been able to preserve its Roman Catholic religion, its French language, and its French laws, free from much contamination by what it regards as Anglo-American secularism, precisely because its people thought of themselves not merely as French but also as Canadians. We give credit to John A. Macdonald, Etienne Cartier, and their successors: but we must always remember that a political leader can lead only because he is followed. Indeed, Carlyle's famous aphorism, 'I am their leader, therefore must I follow them', is very apt. What is needed is not merely a good draftsman, nor even politicians with broad patriotism and tolerant ideas, but also a people capable of appreciating the larger patriotism.

The problems involved are even more clearly exhibited by India, Pakistan and Ceylon. Let us begin with Ceylon because there too problems were simpler and they were solved with none of the troubles which still vex India and Pakistan.

Two-thirds of the population of Ceylon are Sinhalese by race and language and Buddhist by religion. Most of the rest are migrants from India, some of them Hindu and some Muslim. Most of the Hindus are Tamils from South India, speaking Tamil: but some of them migrated centuries ago and are called Ceylon Tamils, while others have migrated since 1840 and are called Indian Tamils. The differences between the Sinhalese and the Tamils are far greater than the differences between the English and the French, or even than between the English and the modern Greeks. Buddhism and Hinduism are tolerant religions, and such conflicts as those which have arisen in India between Hindus and Muslims have not occurred. There were conflicts between Sinhalese and Muslims in 1915, though they were economic as well as religious; but generally the communalism of Ceylon, though pronounced, was unaggressive. What is more, the political leaders, though conscious of their communal origins and dependent on the votes of communally conscious electors, managed to develop the larger patriotism which transcended communalism.

Indeed, when the problem was studied by the Ceylonese themselves in the early 'forties, it became clear that it had been exaggerated. Two Commissions reported on the constitutional problems of Ceylon, the Donoughmore Commission in 1928 and the Soulbury Commission in 1945. Both made pertinent reports, but both exaggerated the communal problem because they came fresh to it. Each minority group wanted to stake a claim for itself, and each exaggerated its claim. When one of the commissions added up all the minority claims, it found that if all were granted there would be no seats for the majority community, the Sinhalese. The claims were always exaggerated because the decision rested with the third party, the British Government: but the claims were especially exaggerated when a commission was in the Island because every politician became an advocate for his own community.

It must not be assumed that there was no communalism: there was and still is. But there was also a larger patriotism. The Ceylonese Ministers produced a compromise scheme, which was reasonably fair to all sections, and then in effect said to the minorities 'Will you have the present dependent Constitution, or will you have this alternative, which does not meet all your claims but is fair to all communities and gives us much more self-government?'. Being nationalists as well as communalists, the minorities agreed, and the vote was almost unanimous. Whitehall was not only surprised but delighted. Some had said that Whitehall's emphasis on the prevalence of communalism was part of the game, a device to hold on to power as long as possible. The allegation proved to be false, and the decision of October 1945 was a very material help towards the last step in constitutional advance, two years later, when Ceylon achieved independence.

The problem in undivided India was far more complicated. It led eventually to the establishment of Pakistan and to all the troubles, for millions of people, which flowed from the partition of India. Those troubles are by no means over. We must remember, however, that the problem of communalism in undivided India was not merely that there was a conflict between Hindus and Muslims. There were difficulties based on caste, and not merely between the scheduled castes and the caste Hindus, but also between Brahmins and Non-Brahmins. Those difficulties are still noticeable in State politics in India. There were difficulties based upon religion apart from those between Hindus and Muslims. There were problems relating to the Sikhs and the Indian Christians. There were even divisions among the Muslims, which are still evident in Pakistan. Some months ago there was bloodshed because of a conflict among Muslim sects and the Constitution of the Punjab had to be suspended. Also, the Muslims of East Bengal have social customs of a secular kind much like those of the Hindus of West Bengal; and it is not very easy for them to form a nation with the Muslims of West Pakistan, whose links are with Muslim Asia, not with India.

There were, and still are, problems relating to linguistic groups. The Indian Constitution provides for thirteen State languages, of which four are Dravidian languages in the south, while nine are Indo-Aryan languages in the north. Efforts are being made to add languages to the list, because there are many languages in India; and, if we count dialects, the number rises to hundreds. Each linguistic group is a community, capable of organising itself into a political group. In Pakistan there has been a long conflict between those who wanted Urdu alone as national language and those who wanted Bengali also. Three more languages may have to be recognised as provincial languages.

This is by no means all. At the beginning of this talk I described the United Kingdom as relatively homogeneous economically. That is not so in Asia. At the one extreme are the poor villagers of India and Pakistan and the slum-dwellers of the great towns. These live in conditions, and at an economic level, which no Englishman would tolerate. At the other extreme are the merchant princes of Bombay and Calcutta, far richer than the richest men in Britain. Nor must one think of the contrast only in economic terms. The great mass of the population of India and Pakistan cannot read, and there would be nothing to read if they could. Unlike the illiterate villagers of Ceylon, they never hear a newspaper read, listen to the radio, or even talk to a person who can read. There are villages to which there are no roads, only tracks across the jungle or the desert, and which have never seen a motor bus or a train. On the other hand are the learned Brahmins and the ablest graduates of the universities.

Even so, I have not yet fully drawn the contrast. In India and Pakistan there are tribes so primitive that culturally they have not progressed much beyond the Stone Age. The anthropologists tell us that their native ability is as great as ours or of their Indian neighbours: but we and their neighbours learn at home from our parents and friends a vast range of accomplishments and a whole complex of ideas which are the product of centuries of development. No doubt conditions can be changed in a few generations; but it takes a great deal of education to remove the consequences of a primitive home and tribal environment.

This contrast between homogeneous Britain and heterogeneous Asia is instructive: but it does not fully exhibit the problem of raising a colony to self-government. Hinduism, Islam and Buddhism are philosophical religions which help to create a range of ideas even among the illiterate villagers. India, Pakistan and Ceylon are the heirs of great traditions, older than and not inferior to those of Europe. No doubt the basic human material is everywhere the same, but the process of self-government depends upon the accumulated wisdom of centuries of development. In India, Pakistan and Ceylon there have been not merely centuries, but thousands of years, of such development.

We must not be led astray by slogans. Those who are trying to maintain 'white supremacy' in Africa do their best to treat the exception as the rule. Because some Africans belong to primitive tribes they suggest that all Africans are primitive. Those who have met African students in London, or who have visited Africa, know that the allegation is nonsense. When I was in Zululand in 1953 I felt that it would not be difficult to sit down with the Zulu elders and an interpreter and work out a Constitution for Zululand. Unfortunately Zululand is not, or at least does not seem to be, a possible political unit, except possibly as a unit of a broader Union of South Africa which enabled Britain and Boer, Bantu and Basuto, Indian and Zulu, to live and work together. Moreover, it is far easier to lay down a general proposition than it is to work out the details and get them accepted. Our task in East Africa is to produce a 'partnership' of European, Indian and African. It is a beautiful phrase and it solves the whole problem—until the constitutional lawyer is brought in to work out the franchise, the number of seats, the methods of election, the rules of parliamentary procedure, the method of appointing a Cabinet, and the thousand other details needed to define 'partnership'. Then we shall discover, as we discoverd in Asia, the meaning of 'communalism'.

One evening in a Government office in Colombo I had a conversation with Mr D. S. Senanayake, who became the first Prime Minister of Ceylon. Discussions were going on whether the Sinhalese should have 50 per cent, or 55 per cent, or 60 per cent, or 65 per cent, of the seats in the Parliament of Ceylon. Mr Senanayake said that we should never solve the problem by that sort of argument, because everybody would haggle like a Sindhi merchant trying to sell a carpet. We needed a principle, a principle which could be defended. I went home with the problem in my mind; at 4 a.m. I woke up with the problem still on my mind; and within half-an-hour I had found a principle which is now incorporated in the Ceylon Constitution. Compared with many of our problems in Africa that was an easy problem. My point is not that there may be a solution, but that the problem of getting a Constitution in a 'plural' society, where there are a great many competing loyalties, where every little community is engaged in haggling, where emotions are as dangerous as Ceylon fireworks, and where everybody who is not a sworn brother is potentially a dangerous enemy, is not simple.

Let me take an example which was relatively simple, though it ended in a war. In California in 1939 I heard an Arab professor make a violent attack on British rule in Palestine, where Britain was the mandatory under the League of Nations. Afterwards he and I were invited to coffee by our American friends. I told him that I had much sympathy with his point of view. Unfortunately an Israeli professor would have made an equally violent attack on the mandatory power, but his conclusion would have been exactly the opposite of that reached by my Arab friend. I asked him whether Britain should deliver Palestine to the Arabs or to the Jews. His indignant reply was that Palestine was not ours to give. For an adequate fee I would have defended the thesis that the decision lay with Britain and the League of Nations: but the point is that this kind of problem was so charged with emotion that a rational solution was difficult if not impossible. In the end the British Government walked out and let the Jews and the Arabs fight it out. The Jews, being more efficient, better organised, and better trained, seized nearly the whole of Palestine. Whether this was the best solution is not within my province to decide: but I doubt whether it is moral, when we are charged with responsibility, to abdicate that responsibility in such a way that thousands of people lose their lives and thousands more lose their homes. Our task, as I see it, is to transfer our responsibilities peacefully and decorously. It is no argument that we ought never to have had those responsibilities. They have been vested in us, and somehow we must solve the problem that they impose.

III

THE UNIT OF GOVERNMENT

ONE way to avoid the difficulties of a plural society is to create units of government which are, so far as may be possible, socially homogeneous. This is exactly the reverse of the process proposed by Lord Durham in 1840 as a solution for the communal problem of Canada. He suggested that if Lower Canada, or Quebec, were combined with Upper Canada, or Ontario, the English would in due course swamp the French. Few prophecies have been more unsuccessful. Constant difficulties arose in United Canada, and those difficulties were not overcome until 1867, when Ontario and Quebec became separate Provinces of the Dominion of Canada.

His recommendation was made before the development of linguistic nationalism in the nineteenth century, the nationalism which created Italy and Germany and, in this century, split the Austro-Hungarian Empire and caused the establishment of the Baltic States. In Europe there has been something of a reaction because national sovereignty is an impediment to international organisation and is the fundamental cause of war. In theory, the Marxists do not accept it at all. The U.S.S.R. has reabsorbed the Baltic States and has converted the rest of Eastern Europe into a collection of satellite States having far less freedom than most British colonies. Old-fashioned nationalism is therefore strongest in the dependent territories and in those territories, like India, Pakistan, Ceylon, Burma and Indonesia, which have recently ceased to be dependent. Unfortunately, there is almost always a conflict of loyalties. In United Canada the division between English and French was based both on language and on religion and it was not difficult to make a territorial division. In Ceylon the division is based on 'race', language and religion, but it is difficult, if not impossible, to make it a political division also. In undivided India the fundamental conflict was in respect of religion and that conflict caused the separation of India and Pakistan. Within both countries, however, there are divisions of 'race', language and religion which complicate the problem of government.

In most of the dependent territories the position is at least as complicated. The Union of South Africa supplies an example of a complex plural society, though it has made no attempt to solve the problem on lines which would be acceptable in the remainder of the Commonwealth. Roughly there are two million Europeans, divided unequally between English-speaking and Afrikaans-speaking. Though the English are more numerous in the Cape and Natal, while the Afrikaners are more numerous in Transvaal and the Orange Free State, it was decided to have a unitary Constitution with substantial devolution to the provinces. Even so there is in Natal a minority movement for a federal Constitution. The ten million non-Europeans include a substantial minority of Indians, who are strongest in Natal. There is also, especially in the Cape, a small minority of what the South Africans call 'coloured people', i.e. Eurasians and Eurafricans of mixed descent. Finally the majority of the population consists of Africans. Many of them live in reserves with their own tribal organisation, and they speak different varieties of the Bantu languages. Others have become detribalised and live in or near the towns.

As I have said, the South Africans have made no

attempt to solve this problem on acceptable lines, for the South African theory of *Apartheid* and racial discrimination could not be accepted elsewhere. My point is, however, that it would be extremely difficult to solve it along acceptable lines. Questions of race, language, economic status, educational development, and even religion are all involved. If the problem were put to the constitutional lawyer as a theoretical problem he might have to suggest constitutional devices of a peculiar and unprecedented character; but it is very doubtful whether those devices would be acceptable; and if they were not acceptable they would be unworkable.

In any case it is evident that a unit of government which is socially homogeneous is impracticable. A complex plural society cannot be divided into a collection of homogeneous units. It is therefore necessary to create a national patriotism which overrides communal loyalties. Countries like Switzerland, Canada, India and Ceylon have shown that it can be done. Clearly we have to accept, and indeed welcome, what I described just now as old-fashioned nationalism. It creates difficulties in international relations, as experience in Asia has shown: but it does provide that 'larger patriotism' which is essential for efficient internal government.

One of the fundamental difficulties in plural societies in the Commonwealth is that while English is the common medium which binds the groups together, it is also the medium which binds the dependency to the United Kingdom. In Canada, English and French have virtually become official languages, though French is really used officially only in Quebec, in the debates of the Canadian Parliament, and in the Supreme Court of Canada. In South Africa, English and Afrikaans are both official languages, and a serious attempt is being made to make everybody bilingual. What happens in practice is that the Afrikaners learn to use both languages almost equally well, while the English South Africans speak English and understand Afrikaans. Equality has therefore not been attained; and, since the English-speaking South Africans are a minority, political conflict results. English is a particularly penetrative language because it is international, and therefore is used far more widely in literature, films and the radio than a local language like Afrikaans can ever be used.

In Asia the problem is even more difficult because English is the language of what used to be the 'ruling race', and it is spoken only by the very small educated section of the population. On the other hand, when once independence has been attained it becomes politically neutral. In Ceylon there have been suggestions for replacing English by Sinhalese. Such suggestions are resented by the minorities, most of whom speak Tamil. It was therefore agreed that both Sinhalese and Tamil should become 'national languages'. The difficulty is that very few Sinhalese speak Tamil and very few Tamils speak Sinhalese; but all educated Ceylonese speak English, which is thus the common language. It is also the medium of instruction at higher educational levels. Consequently, the Sinhalese and the Tamils have to be segregated at the lower educational levels, where communalism necessarily develops. If English is used, Sinhalese and Tamils speak together and play together: when Sinhalese and Tamil are used, racial segregation results and communalism is encouraged.

India has tried to solve this problem by creating one national language, Hindi, but also authorising twelve other regional languages, which are used in the States. Since Hindi is the language of a minority, however, there is passive resistance to its use in some parts of the country, especially in the South, where the four Dravidian languages are spoken. Also, the use of the regional languages in the States necessarily helps to create or strengthen communalism. Indeed, there are demands for a new alignment of the States according to language. The State of Andhra has already been created for the people who speak Telugu and agitation is proceeding for the creation of States capable of using such languages as Kannada, Malayalam, Gujarati, Marathi, Rajasthari, Punjabi and so on. In other words, in spite of the decision to use Hindi as national language, India is tending to split into linguistic segments.

Language is particularly important because it results in communal segregation. Religion is another factor. It is particularly important among Muslims because, though the brotherhood of Islam has been split into nationalist groups—Algeria, Tunisia, Morocco, Egypt, Jordan, Turkey, Saudi Arabia, Iraq, Iran, Afghanistan, Pakistan, Malaya, Indonesia, etc.—it is still very real. Anybody who has lived among Muslims during the fast of Ramazan is compelled to realise how potent is the influence of Islam. In Western Europe, religion is an incident of a secular life, except for those who have been called to a religious life. In Islamic countries everybody is something of a theologian. It was this brotherhood of Islam which brought the Muslims of undivided India together in support of the Muslim League led by the Quaid-i-Azam, Mr Jinnah. History will probably tell us that the Indian National Congress, under the influence of Mahatma Gandhi and Mr Jawaharlal Nehru, was maladroit in its handling of the religious issue. Though fundamentally Hindu, it sought to establish a secular State in which religion should be a purely personal factor. That idea accords with the tolerance and diversity of Hinduism; but it does not accord with the solidarity of Islam. It is probable that, as late as 1945, undivided India could have become a federation of Hindu and Muslim States if the Hindus had realised that the demands of the Muslim League for separate Muslim States with Islamic ideals needed to be met. This would have involved a rather loose federation, in which the Muslim States which were ultimately transferred to Pakistan could achieve their Islamic ideals. Since the Congress refused to accept this differentiation, the creation of Pakistan became inevitable.

Pakistan has proposed to call itself an Islamic Republic and it is Islam which holds it together. A glance at the map shows that East Pakistan and West Pakistan are separated by a thousand miles of Indian territory. The map does not show another factor which is equally important, that racially and linguistically the two sections are equally far apart. The Muslims of West Pakistan are, in the main, the descendants of Muslim invaders from Central Asia, who created the great Mughal Empire. The Muslims of East Pakistan are racially and linguistically akin to the Bengali of West Bengal, an Indian State. Probably they are the descendants of Hindus converted to Islam. Even though millions of Muslim refugees left India when Pakistan was created, and millions of Hindus left Pakistan for India, there are still millions of Muslims in India.

Though it may not have been noticed because I did not stress the point, I have mentioned three methods of solving the communal problem. The first, which is adopted in Ceylon and South Africa, is to achieve a balance between communal ideas, but to form a single State which does its best to develop the larger patriotism. The second method, adopted in the division of British India into India and Pakistan, is to create separate States based on communal differences: India is predominantly Hindu, while Pakistan is predominantly Muslim. The third method, illustrated in Canada, India and Pakistan, is to create a federation of States in such a way that, so far as may be possible, the separate States in the federation can stress their communal loyalties.

This brings us, however, to a very practical problem. What is the effective unit for the purposes of government? It is not very easy to give an answer, because several factors are involved, and different persons emphasise different factors.

In the first place, an independent State must be an economic unit. It will have a currency of its own and it will control its economic life through tariffs, excise duties, exchange control, and other governmental methods. No State can be economically independent, for we are all engaged in taking in each other's washing: but it must be able to maintain its own economy. We have recently had experience in a small country under the protection of the Crown. In the Indian Ocean is a group of islands, called the Maldive Islands, inhabited by a population of 100,000, engaged mainly in fishing. Problems relating to defence and external affairs do not arise because they are handled by the United Kingdom. Subject to these consequences of British protection, however, the Maldives are independent. In 1952, at the request of the then Prime Minister, I drafted a new Constitution for the Maldivians and I was present in Male, the capital island, when the Constitution was proclaimed in Maldivian fashion on the 1 January 1953. Within eight months that Constitution was overthrown by *coup d'état.* The explanation is to be found not in the Constitution but in a rapid deterioration of economic conditions. The prices of the main export, Maldive fish, were low: the prices of imported goods, mainly rice, were high. The result was an adverse balance of payments which was met by the depreciation of the Maldivian rupee. Such a step results inevitably in the lowering of the standard of living of the people. In January 1953, as I saw for myself, the Maldivian people were solidly behind their Government. Eight months later they were ready and anxious for a change because many of them were almost starving. Man cannot live on fish and coconuts alone; and it was essential that the Maldivian Government reform its economic policy so as to make rice and other imported goods available. With the assistance of the Governments of the United Kingdom, Ceylon, India and Pakistan, economic stability was restored. Such stability is essential to effective self-government.

In the second place, a self-governing people must provide for its own defence and the maintenance of its external affairs. So long as a country is a colony, the whole cost of its external affairs and a large part of the cost of its defence is borne by the United Kingdom. The cost of its external relations depends on its situation and its ambitions. India, which at once became a world power, has diplomatic representatives in nearly fifty countries, whereas Ceylon is represented in eight centres only. The cost is in either case proportionately heavy, and, since much of it has to be met in foreign currencies, it is a considerable factor in the balance of payments. The cost of defence is, or may be, even heavier. India spends about 200 crores of rupees, or £150 million, every year, while Pakistan, which is in a particularly dangerous position, has to spend about 40 per cent of its total revenue on its armed forces. Ceylon, on the other hand, spends comparatively little.

Obviously, expenditure on defence depends upon the geographical location of the country concerned, its relationships with friendly countries, and its willingness to take risks. Before 1947, the cost of the defence of India was so heavy that the Congress accused the British Government of using the Indian forces for its 'imperialist adventures'. Since defence figures are rarely published, it is difficult to say whether the forces of India and Pakistan are larger or smaller than those maintained before partition. One of the factors involved is the adoption by the Government of India of a 'neutralist' policy which assumes that India can keep out of any war in which the great powers may be involved. Given the strategic position of India, this is a gamble which may or may not come off. In any case, the first brunt of an attack on India, if it came by land by the easiest route, would be borne by the armed forces of Pakistan. The invention of new methods of warfare has not altered the strategic pattern for actual invasion, which must come through the Khyber Pass. Nor can either India or Pakistan forget its most intimate neighbour, especially so long as the problem of Kashmir remains unsolved. Indeed, the first assignment of the Indian army was the occupation of as much of Kashmir as could be wrested from the tribesmen pouring in from Pakistan. Almost immediately afterwards it was called upon to take 'police action' in Hyderabad. Adventures of this kind used to be called by harsher names; but they are not inconsistent with the strident nationalism which develops in opposition to British rule; and the disappearance of *Pax Britannica* will in most cases increase the cost of defence.

In spite of the division of the Indian army in 1947 India and Pakistan could rely mainly upon local officers, though probably some ten or twelve years will elapse before the last British officer leaves the subcontinent. They have also to rely, for the time being, on

British training facilities, though eventually both sets of armed forces will be large enough to provide for their own training, except in highly specialised armaments. Similarly, the demands for equipment are large enough to justify local production, except of highly specialised types. For instance, India is now producing electronic, radio and radar equipment. It will soon be able to build small warships. More complicated equipment has to be purchased abroad and, since it is expensive, the drain on foreign exchange resources is considerable.

India is, however, a special case because of its size. The experience of Ceylon is more relevant. When the question of the independence of Ceylon was under discussion between 1943 and 1947, the problem of defence loomed very large. By 1942 the Japanese were in occupation of the eastern side of the Bay of Bengal from Burma to Sumatra, including the Andaman and Nicobar Islands. The Japanese fleet dominated the Bay; in April 1942 Ceylon had been raided by bombers from Japanese aircraft carriers and it could have been occupied without much difficulty; later on the island was within range of long-distance bombers based on Malaya and the Andaman Islands; Japanese submarines operated in the waters around the coasts of the island. History does not repeat itself exactly, but it was obvious that an independent Ceylon could not defend itself in a war which extended to the Indian Ocean and that its strategic position was too important for it to hope for neutrality.

It was feared by the Ceylonese leaders that this strategic weakness would be used as an argument against the grant of independence. There was at least a case for asserting, as Britain had done in May 1943, that Ceylon should have full internal self-government, but with control of defence and external affairs retained by the United Kingdom. In answer to this case it was decided to offer the United Kingdom a defence agreement under which the United Kingdom would be ensured a friendly but independent Ceylon. The scheme was rejected in 1945, apparently because the problem of India had not been solved; and when the problem was again discussed in 1947, after the promise of independence to India and Burma, Ceylon was not prepared to offer so much. A new agreement was then negotiated between Sir Oliver Goonetilleke and the United Kingdom Government, which was signed in Colombo in November 1947. Under it the United Kingdom has naval and air bases in Ceylon and provides training facilities for the armed forces of Ceylon. On the other hand, Ceylon is not bound to provide bases for the United Kingdom. If it chooses to undertake the whole burden of defence—which would be economically impossible unless it was prepared to gamble on its neutrality being recognised by the belligerents—it can do so.

It is impossible to generalise about these matters because the position of every dependent territory is peculiar. Ceylon's position on all the sea routes into the Bay of Bengal and on the most important sea routes and air routes between Suez on the one side and the Far East and Australia on the other, is necessarily weak in wartime. On the other hand, all the other members of the Commonwealth—including even the Union of South Africa, whose east coast route might be interrupted from Ceylon—are interested in maintaining the independence of a friendly Ceylon. Accordingly, in this respect Ceylon does not provide much of a precedent for application elsewhere. Nevertheless, the example does show the importance of ability to undertake self-defence. Incidentally too, it shows the importance of having political leaders who are prepared frankly to face and to seek to overcome the difficulties in the way of independence.

In the third place, the territory must be such that the country can govern itself efficiently. Exactly what this means I do not know. When a constitutional lawyer is asked to recommend political institutions for any political entity, be it a city like Singapore or Hong Kong, a fortress like Malta or Gibraltar, an island like Cyprus or a West Indian colony, or a collection of islands like the Maldives or the West Indies, it is not his business to say that it cannot be done. Indeed it can be done. What one ought not to do is to produce an array of governmental authorities out of proportion to the population involved. The cost of government has to be met out of the productivity of the people. A small country cannot support a great hierarchy of politicians and officials.

Let us take a hypothetical example. Suppose we have a country of four million people, divided into four quarters of one million each, each quarter containing people of a different race or religion. One might have a unitary government with some measure of devolution to the four quarters, as in South Africa: or one might have a more expensive but perhaps more acceptable federal Constitution: or one might divide up the State and convert it into four States. It is impossible to say which is the best solution, because it depends on local sentiment, economic conditions, and so on. If, however, we take a much smaller place so that each quarter contains not one million but one thousand people, it is plain that a very simple structure must be created. A federal Constitution, with five legislatures and five governments would be out of the question. Everybody would spend the taxes and nobody would pay them.

It must also be remembered that a small country has

to undertake all the services of a large country, but with a much smaller and simpler organisation. In a large country like the United Kingdom there can be a division of labour, so that every aspect of government can be handled by an expert in that particular field. A small country cannot afford such a vast array of experts; every official has to be an adaptable person capable of handling a variety of jobs. What is more, he has to do without much of the technical equipment which would be available in a larger country. Even in fields like education, in which there is a large *cadre* upon which to draw, Pakistan as well as Ceylon suffers from a deficiency of highly skilled personnel. Nor can the necessary training be obtained by sending persons to the United States or the United Kingdom, or even to Canada or Australia, because neither country can manage its services as they are managed in those countries: the expert personnel and the technical equipment are not available and cannot be made available because of the cost involved. The Pakistani or Ceylonese administrator has to 'make do' in a manner which he cannot learn in a more highly organised country. The Government of Ceylon once asked me to report on school broadcasting in the United Kingdom—it was typical of a small country that the vice-chancellor of the University of Ceylon, who was by profession a constitutional lawyer, should be asked to undertake such an investigation. It at once became clear to me that very little could be learned from the United Kingdom, not because the B.B.C. had nothing to teach, but because the Ceylon broadcasting authorities could not draw upon one-hundredth of the resources in men, materials and money upon which the B.B.C. relied. To have recommended anything like the B.B.C. system would have been out of all proportion to the scale of government possible in Ceylon. It was necessary to plan an organisation within the limited resources available. This was a minor illustration of a general problem. A small country like Ceylon cannot duplicate the Foreign Office, or even the Ministry of External Affairs in New Delhi; for all practical purposes two persons, a Secretary and an Assistant Secretary, have to handle matters of foreign policy from China to Peru.

Thus, it is useless to argue that there are, in the public service of 'Arcadia', people as able as those in the public service of the United Kingdom. Actually, there are not, because the competition both inside and outside the public service is much less keen. The best of five hundred graduates are not so good as the best of five thousand graduates, even if the educational system is equally good, because competition pushes up the standard; the best of five thousand administrators are not so good as the best of fifty thousand administrators, for the same reason. A person's capacity is not something fixed by his I.Q., it is stretched by his experience and his competitors. In any case, a different type is required; there have to be more general administrators and fewer technical experts, and the general administrator has to learn to take sensible decisions without the barrage of expert advice that he would receive in a larger administration. In Ceylon the present Secretary to the Treasury was formerly Permanent Secretary to the Ministry of Education; before that he was Director of Agriculture; I first knew him as a Deputy Commissioner in charge of the purchase of paddy; and before that, I believe, he was a district officer in one of the Provinces. This is not an unusual career, for it is a tradition taken over from the colonial service and it is necessary in colonial administration because no colony can afford to carry a large staff on its exiguous revenues. The question to be decided in each case is, of course, how far this kind of dilution can be carried without making the process of administration so inefficient that independence cannot be justified.

Finally, the country must be able to secure the loyalty of its citizens. If they are sharply divided, as the Hindus were divided from the Muslims in India in 1947, it may be necessary to create separate States. On the other hand, history has shown us that it is possible for people of different races and religions to work together if stable institutions can once be established and a common loyalty developed. Moreover, the communities are rarely separated geographically in such a manner that separate communal units can be established. In some parts of Africa, including the Union, there are three distinct communal groups, the Europeans, the Indians and the Africans. One may argue whether Kenya, Uganda and Tanganyika should be combined, or whether the Rhodesias and Nyasaland should be combined: but one could not divide Kenya into European, Indian and African segments.

These are generalities which may help the listener to appreciate the complexity of the problem, but they do not help much when a practical problem has to be solved—such a problem, let us say, as Closer Union in East Africa or the Central African Federation. Experience in Asia suggests that arm-chair discussion can rarely produce useful results. A modern Jeremy Bentham must take a 'plane to Mexico and learn something about the country and its people, and especially about their emotions. The problem of the unit of government is particularly difficult because there is no certain solution. Nearly forty years ago a Professor of Political Science who was also President of the United States, President Wilson, enunciated a doctrine which was ridiculous, but which was widely accepted as a sensible proposition, the doctrine of self-determination. On the surface it seemed reasonable: let the people decide. It was in fact ridiculous because the people cannot decide until somebody decides who are the people.

Let us take an example which comes very near home, the United Kingdom of Great Britain and Ireland as it was in the nineteenth century. The people of the United Kingdom had self-government, but some of them said that Ireland ought to have Home Rule. Who was to decide that: the people of the United Kingdom, the people of Great Britain, or the people of Ireland? There was great argument on that very point between the Conservative and Liberal parties. Even so, we have simplified the problem. Most of the Irish representatives in Parliament said that Ireland should decide: but why Ireland? Ireland was not necessarily a political unit because it happened to be an island. In fact, we know that the majority of people in three Provinces wanted Ireland to have Home Rule, while the majority of people in Ulster wanted Ireland to remain in the United Kingdom. But why regard Ulster as a unit? There were counties in Ulster which wanted Home Rule for Ireland and counties which did not. But why take counties, why not towns and villages; and why towns and villages instead of streets and homes? If one really consults the people, the conclusion may be that in the town of Londonderry fifteen streets and a quarter and five isolated houses shall belong to the Republic of Ireland and the rest to the United Kingdom.

We might, of course, have asked President Wilson to take another example. If the people of the Northern States want to be the United States, and the people of the Southern States want to form a separate Confederation of States, who is to decide, the people of the United

States, the people of the Northern States, or the people of the Southern States? It is not very clear what President Wilson meant; but it is reasonably clear that President Abraham Lincoln would not have agreed with him, though possibly President Washington would. One wonders, too, whether President Eisenhower would approve of the State of Texas deciding to exercise the right of self-determination and to join the Union of Soviet Socialist Republics.

Problems of this kind cannot be solved by the application of academic principles. The wishes or emotions of any particular group, such as the Roman Catholics of Ireland, or the inhabitants of Texas, or the Muslims of India, or the Indians of Kenya, must be taken into consideration. It is not possible, however, to satisfy everybody. In South Africa, for instance, there are Afrikaners, English-speaking South Africans, Indians and Africans. Even these are generic names, and the various groups of Africans may well have different ideas. The principle of the majority works very well where there is a homogeneous population, as in Great Britain. It cannot be applied in a plural society. For instance, it is clear that the problem of Kenya cannot be solved by a majority vote, though equally it cannot be solved by the European inhabitants without consideration of the opinions of the Indians and the Africans. It is a difficult problem for which, probably, there is no ideal solution. We must not, however, leap to the opposite conclusions and assume that there is no solution. There is no problem of government that cannot be solved by goodwill; and if goodwill is lacking one must take steps to create it. My experience in Asia has made me an optimist. Everywhere in the world there are stupid people, and quite often one finds that the stupid people do most of the talking: but the ordinary person in every part of the Commonwealth, and indeed of the world, is a very sensible person. He is, too, a tolerant person. If a problem is explained to him, and if he is convinced that the person giving the explanation has no axe to grind, he will do his best to help towards a sensible solution. By the accident of history, the people of Hornsey, Huddersfield, Hertford, Pontypool, Gorbals, Hamilton and Londonderry—to take examples entirely at random—have become responsible for the welfare of millions of people in the colonies. If they can be persuaded that the people of the Gold Coast and Nigeria, British Honduras and Hong Kong, Basutoland and British North Borneo, are much like them, it is not impossible to reach a sensible decision. The pragmatism of the British people is a helpful characteristic. If every problem is regarded as a practical problem, we constitutional lawyers can produce a practicable solution. Sometimes, in moments of exasperation, one realises how easy political problems would become if there were no politicians.

IV

ELECTIONS

THE homogeneity of the United Kingdom, to which I have to keep drawing attention, makes the problem of organising elections an easy one. We assume that every adult is entitled to the franchise and that his voice should be as effective as that of any other voice. Accordingly the country is divided by an impartial commission into constituencies each containing roughly the same number of electors. The division is not exact. In particular Northern Ireland has fewer constituencies than its population would warrant because it also has its own Parliament sitting in Belfast, while Wales and Scotland have rather more, so as not to make the rural constituencies too large. Even in England there is variation between the 39,000 electorate of Battersea South and the 77,000 electorate of Hornchurch. Mathematical accuracy is impossible, not only because population is always on the move but also because one must pay attention to physical and communal boundaries. The Isle of Wight must have either one member or two members: it would not be sensible to give it one-and-a-half. Bristol must have either four members or five.

Another characteristic of elections in the United Kingdom is that we can and do assume that every elector can read the literature which is sent him by the candidates, can find out where his polling station is, can read the notices which direct him to the appropriate room, and can read and mark a ballot paper correctly. Finally, as I pointed out in my first talk, homogeneity leads to a party system which is the same throughout the country. Land's End is in the St Ives division of Cornwall, which is represented by a Conservative. John o' Groats is in Caithness and Sutherland, which is also represented by a Conservative.

These characteristics are not to be found in the Asian countries of the Commonwealth, and they are not likely to be found in Africa or the West Indies. Let us begin with the simplest problem, that of the mechanics of voting. An illiterate elector cannot be expected to be able to distinguish the names on a ballot paper even if he can learn to hold a pencil and make some sort of a mark. Between 1931 and 1947 Ceylon used the method of the coloured ballot box. Each candidate was given a colour, red or green or yellow or blue, and each polling booth contained a set of ballot boxes each painted in the appropriate colour. The voter received a ballot paper from the presiding officer, entered the booth, and dropped his paper into the box painted with the colour allocated to his candidate. It was found that there were difficulties in this arrangement. Contrasted colours had to be used because one cannot have, for instance, royal blue and Oxford blue. Unfortunately, some colours have special associations. Yellow is the Buddhist colour, green the Muslim colour, and red has a political significance all the world over. In a Buddhist constituency everybody wanted yellow, even the 'leftist' who flew the red flag over his party headquarters, because it was easy to persuade the illiterate voter to vote for Buddhism. Hence lots had to be drawn: but this might mean that the virulent anti-communist had to fly a red flag.

The principal difficulty, however, was that the system lent itself to traffic in ballot-papers. William Singho would collect his ballot paper and enter the booth, but he then tucked his ballot paper into his cloth and went outside, where an agent of a rich candidate would give him two rupees, or perhaps as much as five rupees, for his ballot paper. Later on, when a wad of ballot papers had been collected in this way, another voter would be sent in, with the wad in his pocket. He would collect his ballot paper, enter the booth and drop into the appropriate ballot box not only the ballot paper that he had just received, but also the wad from his pocket.

The method now used in most Asian elections is the symbol. Each candidate is allocated a symbol which is easily distinguished even by an illiterate voter, but which has no ideological significance, such as an elephant, a house, a key, a pair of scales, a bicycle, an eye, or something of that kind. In India and Pakistan the symbol is shown on the ballot box, and each candidate has his own box in each polling booth; in effect this is the same as the older Ceylon method and has the same danger in respect of traffic in ballot papers. Also, since the ballot papers are unmarked, but the votes cast for a candidate depend upon the number of papers in his box, it has been alleged that insertion of ballot papers into the box during or after the poll is not a difficult matter. The precautions laid down in electoral laws ought to be sufficient; and if it is easy to insert unmarked ballot papers it ought to be almost as easy to insert marked ballot papers where the British method is used.

Ceylon has now reverted to the British system of the marked ballot paper, which has to be placed in the ballot box placed in front of the presiding officer. To meet the case of the illiterate voter, the candidate's symbol is placed against the candidate's name. It has not been found difficult to instruct voters orally how to put some sort of mark against a symbol, and of course the symbol is widely advertised by the candidate. In

Indonesia, however, the elector is not expected to make a mark: he is given an instrument by means of which he can push a hole through the ballot paper against the symbol of the candidate for whom he wishes to vote. There have not been many spoilt papers, except in two-member constituencies, where the voter is given two papers. He sometimes imagines that he has to make two marks on each of the two papers, and thus spoils both of them.

There are, too, difficulties over the symbols, because it is difficult to arrange that members of the same party have the same symbol in neighbouring constituencies. In Ceylon the allocation of symbols is determined by lot, with the result that the Government candidate in one constituency may have the same symbol as the Opposition candidate in the next constituency, and thus there is confusion at the border. In India, on the other hand, the returning officer allocates the symbols according to the candidates' preferences, and the central organisation of each party indicates to its candidates which symbol should be selected. This is possible, however, only in single-member constituencies in which each candidate nominates one candidate only. In one Ceylon election where the selection of party candidates proved particularly difficult, one party actually nominated five candidates for one seat.

These methods assume a static urban or village population, among whom constituencies can be delineated and registers of electors drawn up. There are, however, in parts of the Commonwealth nomadic tribes, taking their camels or goats from oasis to oasis, or following the track of the annual rains. Sometimes they cross international boundaries. For instance, there are tribes which cross the borders of the Sudan and Eritrea every year. How is one to get such tribes to the poll? The answer is that one must give up several of the ideas which derive from twentieth-century Britain. In Britain the individual is the unit. Until 1832 British people thought in terms not of individuals but of communities. The House of Commons is historically the House of *communes*, *communitates*, or communities. Our present individualism is the product partly of the ideology of the French Revolution, and partly of the break-up of the mediaeval village by the trek to the towns caused by the factory system. Elsewhere it is still important to think in terms of communities. Representation has to be given not to the tribesman but to the tribe: and the African tribe, like the Anglo-Saxon tribe, has its own method of electing representatives. Probably it sits in a coconut or date grove, with the chief at the centre of the semi-circle, the elders seated in the inner circle and the young men standing in the circumference. If the chief is told to have a representative sent to the nearest town, a representative will arrive; and when the representatives are all present the returning officer can hold a palaver or parliament to decide who shall saddle his camel and go off to represent the tribes in the legislature. This is not election according to the Ballot Act, but it is at least as effective.

So far we have assumed that the illiterate villager and the nomadic tribesman ought to have the vote; but that is one of the problems that have to be settled. Britain never had these problems because the franchise was extended gradually. We have all been subjected to Whig history, which emphasised the anomalies of the unreformed Constitution as it existed in 1830. It was, however, not an unreasonable system in the days of Queen Anne. The resident landowner or squire, the lord of the manor, was as truly the leader of the village as the African chief is the leader of his tribe. When the

Queen summoned a Parliament the squires rode off to the county town to elect two persons to represent the men of the county. There the leadership was taken by the noble lord, or the two or more noble lords, to whom the smaller landlords deferred. There was no contest unless two or more noble lords were fighting for supremacy. Everybody was satisfied, the freeholders dined at the expense of the noble lords, and returned to their villages highly gratified that, by the favour of the noble lords, the Queen should have such excellent county representatives in Parliament.

The county representatives were almost invariably the best people, in a double sense. Less worthy people, the younger sons of noble lords, or the sons or relatives of less noble lords, had to be candidates for boroughs. A fairly large and wealthy borough might wish to send one burgess to Parliament, but it was usually glad to accept the nominee of a neighbouring lord as its second candidate. Less important boroughs, which did not wish to put themselves to the expense of sending and maintaining a Member of Parliament, would be glad to put both seats at the disposal of the great man or great men of the neighbourhood. What is more, it made little difference whether the franchise was vested in the mayor and corporation, or in the holders of specified pieces of land, or in all taxpaying householders, or even in the general body of male citizens: the result was the same.

To our more modern ideas, this sounds like a caricature of representation; but the Tudor and Stuart Parliaments, and even the post-Revolution Parliaments, were at least as representative of the people of England as the Parliaments of the twentieth century. The system of representation accorded with our social system in the early years of the eighteenth century, while the system of representation now in operation accords with our present social system. Even in the early years of the nineteenth century there were people ready to defend the 'mixed' Constitution provided by a hereditary monarch, a hereditary peerage, and a diversified representative system. Nevertheless, the growth of the industrial areas had thrown the system out of balance, and a moderate reform was accepted, rather reluctantly, in 1832. Modern individualistic notions were not accepted until the urban householders were enfranchised in 1867. After that the adoption of household franchise and single-member constituencies was only a question of time. Even so, adult male suffrage was not accepted until 1918, and adult female suffrage only in 1928. In 1945 there were still people with two votes, and still twelve towns represented by two members, as in the Middle Ages.

This outline of history teaches us to beware of the assumption that our present electoral arrangements are necessarily suited to the very diverse conditions of colonial territories. Jim Johnson may be in Honiton this year and in Halifax next year. He expects to have the same influence on the House of Commons when he is in Halifax as when he was in Honiton. Jim Johnson is, as the lawyers put it, 'the man on the Clapham omnibus', the ordinary reasonable man. He is a citizen of Honiton or Halifax by the accident of his employment. That kind of idea does not prevail in a static society, where 'one man, one vote, one value' has no connection with social conditions. A narrow franchise, indirect elections, tribal representation, may all be quite sensible ideas in colonial conditions; and they should not be rejected merely because they are regarded as primitive in Conservative Party Headquarters or Transport House.

It is nevertheless true that in most parts of the Commonwealth society is no longer static. The fondness for roads, which the British like the ancient Romans always exhibit, the use of the motor bus and the bicycle, the prospect of a higher standard of living through migration to the towns or work in mines and factories, even the system of taxation which encourages paid labour, are breaking down the system of subsistence agriculture upon which the old, static social system was founded. I remember going into a hut in a Zulu kraal. There was an iron bedstead, with a mattress, opposite the door. By it was a table with an alarm clock and cutlery. Near the door was a bicycle. Across the hut was a line carrying a couple of clean shirts and a coat hanger keeping a natty pin-striped suit in shape. The Zulu who spoke to us was very much like Jim Johnson, though probably his great-grandfather took part in the battle with the Voortrekkers at Blood River.

The question which arises, therefore, is usually not whether tribal representation is the correct rule to follow, but whether the franchise should be restricted to those who have a substantial income or own a substantial amount of property, or read and write English, or are literate in some other language. There is more in this problem than meets the eye, for any such restricted franchise may achieve a communal balance. In Africa, for instance, it will enfranchise all the Europeans, some of the Indians, and a few of the Africans. We must not complicate the issue at this stage by discussing representation in a plural society; but it should be noted that, in consequence of this process, an educated or wealthy African tends to be a democrat. There is no harm in property or literary qualifications for membership of the legislature, because he is qualified for election: but the more African voters there are the more chance he has of being elected and the greater his power when he is elected. The line between democrat and demagogue is rather fine, and the demagogue is likely to be more common than the solid, cautious conservative who still exists in Britain and in Asia and who, in the opinion even of democrats, contributes an element of stability and caution to political life. The left wing always needs a right wing to give it balance; and, as we shall see, a newly enfranchised colony may tend to be all left-wing.

For the moment, however, we must consider this problem not in communal terms, but in terms of straight representation. In other words, we assume a communally homogeneous electorate. Ceylon achieved adult franchise in 1931 and was, I believe, the first colony to do so. The problem was much discussed before 1931, and was examined by a Commission in 1928. It may therefore be useful to follow the argument as it developed in Ceylon. I propose to ignore the problem of Indian estate labour, which was very controversial but essentially communal.

Under the Constitution of 1924 only 4 per cent of the population had the vote, because the elector had (*a*) to be able to read and write English, Sinhalese or Tamil, and (*b*) to have an annual income of Rs 600 (£50) or own property valued at Rs 1500 (£120), or occupy premises valued at Rs 400 (£30) in an urban area or Rs 200 (£15) in a rural area. The Ceylonese who were arguing for an increased measure of self-government, and who possessed these qualifications, did not recommend any widening of the franchise. It was the Donoughmore Commission of 1928 which insisted that any extension of self-government must be accompanied by an extension of the franchise.

Their main reason was that any extension of self-government, without an equivalent extension of the franchise, would tend to create a middle-class oligarchy. The Commission did not accept the view that it would increase corruption and manipulation of the electorate; in their opinion these practices became more difficult when the electorate was enlarged. An age qualification of 25 was not accepted, because 21 was the age everywhere accepted and some young men already had the vote. The income qualification of Rs 50 a month excluded the great mass of the population, and in particular it cut out most of the villagers and the low-caste workers, who in fact needed representation more than the higher income groups. The literacy qualification was more attractive, but ability to read and write was no test of political judgment: the illiterate villager with his 'horse-sense' might be shrewder and wiser than a city mediocrity. Since education was not available to 45 per cent of the children, it seemed hard that those who were deprived of education should also be deprived of the vote. Above all, no literacy test could ever be satisfactorily administered to a huge potential electorate. Hence the Commission decided for manhood suffrage.

There is a story about this which I must tell, though it is almost certainly apocryphal, because it might have happened to Jeremy Bentham if he had gone to Mexico on a Royal Commission. It was said that the Commission was driving to Kandy with some Ceylonese who were anxious for adult suffrage, and a discussion arose about the intelligence of the villagers. It happened that the cars were passing a group of villagers working in a paddy-field, and it was decided to stop to find out what replies they gave to questions asked by the Commission, the Ceylonese politicians acting as interpreters. It was found that they were remarkably intelligent and had quite a wide knowledge of public affairs. The Commission then drove on, convinced that the villagers indeed had a great deal of horse-sense; but then the 'villagers' left the paddy-field, went to the rest-house to change into coat and trousers, and drove back to Colombo in their own cars.

There had been no substantial demand for votes for women. The Report mentions a 'large and representative delegation of Ceylonese ladies' who asked for the franchise. We now know how that large and representative delegation came into existence. One of the Commissioners asked an unusually emancipated Ceylonese lady whether she was not in favour of votes for women. When she replied that she was, she was asked why she did not organise a delegation to ask for the vote. She collected some who were as emancipated as herself, some who had given no thought to the problem but thought themselves (quite correctly) to be as intelligent as their husbands, and some who did not care whether they had votes or not, but thought it would be amusing to become representative of the womanhood of the Island: the result was the large and representative delegation, chosen by one charming but very unrepresentative lady. At that time it was not in the oriental tradition for women to take an active part in public life, though the process of emancipation was just beginning in India and Ceylon. The process has continued rapidly in the present generation. The Commission was therefore in the van of a great social development: it recommended votes for women at 30, as in Britain between 1918 and 1928. When the Ceylonese found that the electorate was going to be multiplied nine times, they saw no particular reason why it should not be multiplied ten or eleven times: their emancipated daughters for whom husbands were just being sought were hardly likely to abuse the franchise more than the illiterate villager and his discreet wife; and so Ceylon led Asia by adopting adult franchise in 1931.

It will have been noticed that there was some discussion about the possibility of corruption at elections. The Commission gave the answer that an enlargement of the franchise would make corrupt practices more difficult. No doubt the Commission had in mind that, as the franchise was extended in Britain over the past century, corruption of the kind caricatured by Charles Dickens in his description of the election at Eatanswill has gradually disappeared. This is, however, a very partial view of history. The Commission might equally have concluded from the history of democracy in the United States that the more widely the franchise is spread the more corruption there is. Corruption depends not only on the size of the electorate but also on the efficiency of the machinery for maintaining law and order, the degree to which responsibility is concentrated in the political leaders, the sense of responsibility of those who run the party machines, not only on the Government side but also among the smaller parties, the general standard of honesty in the country, and generally the traditions of behaviour. The British Constitution, by concentrating responsibility upon the leaders of a few large parties, none of whom is averse from discovering motes or even beams in his opponents' eyes, by creating a high standard of obedience to law throughout the country, and by having a strong and virtually incorruptible system of law enforcement, has done more to eradicate corruption than by increasing the number of persons who would have to be corrupted. British elections are won and lost in the marginal constituencies, where a few hundred votes make all the difference. The almost equal division of the great mass of the electors between two great parties actually encourages corruption, for it is not the mass of the votes but the very small margins which matter. The fact that there has been no accusation of corruption for half a century is therefore not due to the size of the electorate.

One cannot hope to reach such a situation in Asia or

Africa quickly, and certainly the enlargement of the franchise will not do it. The average elector will take time to learn that his vote is a civic privilege and not a source of profit. Parties are likely for generations to be groups of ambitious politicians rather than mass movements; and though ambition is not a sin it takes time to learn that it is better to lose virtuously than to win viciously. The party leaders who win independence are almost invariably men of courage and probity, but many of their followers are persons who have jumped on the bandwagon, in the belief that after independence politics will be a more profitable occupation than, say, practice at the Bar. The tradition of obedience to law is not well established: indeed, if illegal action is part of the process of 'fighting for freedom' the tradition of disobedience may well be established—India still suffers severely from the civil disobedience movement, for it is not easy for Congress leaders to persuade the young men that disobedience by the Congress was a virtue, while disobedience to the Congress is a vice. Nor is the process of law enforcement in Asia so efficient in Asia as it is in Britain, and allegations that politicians use the police and other public servants to win elections for them are not uncommon. All this is not surprising: there are large parts of the world outside the Commonwealth which have never seen an honest election.

Let me mention some of the problems which have arisen in Asia, at the same time emphasising that the efficiency of elections varies from country to country, from place to place, and from time to time, so that my examples must not be regarded as typical of every country and of every election. The cumulative effect of the examples will therefore be much worse than the facts warrant. Probably most elections are won by honest and lawful means. After one election in Asia the successful candidate observed to his defeated opponent: 'You know, Henry, you ought not to do this kind of thing: you can't win against rogues like me.' It does not follow that all successful candidates are rogues; and indeed this was a very exceptional case, for the successful candidate claimed to be a rogue instead of a true representative of the People with a capital P. There is some truth in the Pathan's remark that 'when Abdul mentions the People he is up to mischief and I reach for my gun'.

First, it is very difficult to secure an accurate register of electors. One must not think of an English town or village, where everybody has a home and is known to his neighbours. Many people in Asia have no homes. A rickshaw puller will probably sleep in his rickshaw, a carter may put his bullock to pasture on somebody else's grass and himself sleep under his cart. Many people sleep on other people's verandahs, with or without the permission of the occupier of the bungalow; and nobody ever knows how many people are sleeping in his compound or who they are. There are nomads who carry their tents on the backs of their camels and who may be enumerated in three constituencies or in none at all. In some cities people sleep in the streets because they are cooler and more comfortable. Even among the people who do sleep in the same place every night there are not necessarily distinguishing names. It may not be clear whether there are nineteen or twenty people named Ramaswamy, and it is quite impossible to identify them. Sons and daughters do not necessarily take the names of their fathers, and some fathers could not recognise their own children, while few could be even reasonably accurate about their ages. Wives do not necessarily take the names of their husbands, and indeed many 'marriages' are not registered. There are men with several wives and even women with several husbands, for polygamy and polyandry are not always unlawful and anyhow the law is not always observed. The mobility of labour is very considerable, so that a servant may be here today and gone tomorrow, nobody knows whither. Every large city has a floating population of labourers who earn what they can where they can.

In Britain the householder fills up a form, listing all the people who are qualified to vote by age and length of residence. There are forms in Asia, too, but most householders cannot read or write. Those who can read and write may not know the particular language in which the form is expressed, and the person who compiles the forms which are transferred to the register may not know the only language in which the elector can write. Registration of births is, in many places, purely optional, and many people do not know their own or their children's ages. They can sometimes remember that little Rukmani was born after the great flood, but whether that makes her 20 or 21 is a matter of argument.

The most efficient system of registration could not cope with all these difficulties, and the system is rarely efficient. Far away in the great capital city is the Election Commission, carefully chosen for its impartiality. A hundred miles away in the big town is the Regional Commissioner who perhaps (and perhaps not, for his future depends on politicians) does his best. The register is compiled by a host of temporary clerks, who earn a little extra money in the evenings by going round collecting the names of the People with a capital P. They get paid the same whether they collect 150 names or 120, or whether they put down 'Raman' or 'Rasaiah', or whether they decide out of hand that Rukmani does not deserve the vote or spend a long time examining exactly what is her claim. Nor is a young man very welcome when he wants to ascertain how many young women there are in the purdah quarters and what their ages are. If he insisted on having the women paraded for his inspection—and he would be a very bold young man—he would probably see a collection of *burqas* whose occupants might be 15 or 50.

So far, I have assumed the honesty of all the officials concerned; but one cannot assume that the young man has no axe to grind, or that his supervisor is honest, or even that the Regional Commissioner has no preferences. They are all public servants whose future depends upon their political superiors. In many cases it is known how individual electors will vote, for they will, unless they are bribed, vote for candidates of their own race, religion and caste. If the local 'boss' is a caste Hindu, it is obviously wise to keep off the register as many as possible of the scheduled castes, especially if they are Christians. If a big zamindar produces a list of twenty persons living in his compound, nobody is likely to be foolish enough to ask how many dogs, goats and bullocks have been included. If it is decided at a high level that 100 names shall be introduced into one register and 100 names deleted from another, the matter is *res judicata;* and indeed the example suggests a parity of reasoning unusual at high political levels.

Perhaps at this point I should produce the second difficulty, though logically it comes later. At the poll at Hammersmith South, John Jones appears before the presiding officer, says he is John Jones of 3 Acacia Villas, and receives his ballot paper accordingly. Oddly enough, to those who have seen elections in some other countries, he really is John Jones, he does live in Acacia Villas, and he is entitled to a ballot paper. There are polling agents whose job it is to challenge his vote if they think he is impersonating someone, but the job is a sinecure. In Asia, John's *alter ego* produces a voting card issued by one of the candidates, purporting to show that he is one of the persons whose name appears on the register. The presiding officer and the polling agents have not the slightest idea whether he really is that person or whether he is one of the zamindar's goats. He takes his ballot paper and he casts his vote for the candidate who gave him the card, and he then goes outside to collect the two rupees payable to an impersonator. If he has assumed the name of a genuine elector, the genuine elector will perhaps come along later and be regarded with the utmost suspicion. Probably he will get out as soon as he can lest he be accused of impersonation: but if he proves truculent he will be given a ballot paper which will be set aside as a 'tendered ballot paper' and never be heard of again.

Impersonation is easy and can be organised on a large scale because of the imperfections of the register and because a person who finds that somebody has already voted in his name is too afraid of police and bureaucrats to make a fuss about it. One method is a revised version of the old English practice of 'polling the dead men'. A thorough canvass will disclose what persons whose names appear on the register are not likely to vote because there never were such persons, or because they are women too modest to appear in public, or because they are dead, or because they have ceased to be resident. Cards setting out the names, addresses and electoral numbers of these persons can be prepared, and given to a posse of impersonators. Indeed the whole process is so easy that, in an urban constituency, it is possible to save the trouble and expense of the canvass, to make out cards at random, and to poll the impersonators early in the day before the genuine electors appear.

It should be said that this form of impersonation is rare in rural constituencies, where the identity of most electors is known. Where purdah is practised, however, it is not difficult to organise impersonation at the women's polling booths. Most purdah women would be far too modest to venture upon such a public act as casting a vote; few of them would be known to the female polling officers imported from the towns; and those who did vote would be so heavily veiled as to be unrecognisable or so covered with their *burqas* that they could not be identified. It is said that at one election a bus-load of women in *burqas* polled 640 votes.

The Ballot Act, if administered properly by honest officials, makes the system of election efficient, accurate and genuine. If it is not so administered it is as full of holes as a mosquito net. Before 1947 a British officer was being examined to discover his knowledge of colloquial Pushto. He was told to ask five tribesmen whether, if a man had 200 rupees, he ought to buy a rifle or a wife. The tribesmen obviously thought the question silly and replied that of course he ought to buy a rifle. Asked why a rifle was to be preferred to a wife, they replied that with a rifle one could get a wife, but with a wife one could not get a rifle. Pressed to explain, they pointed out that if a man had a rifle he could abduct a wife, or rob a caravan and buy a wife. This attitude to law and order is not peculiar to the Frontier. It would not occur to the candidate for Parliament that the easiest way to get elected was to kidnap the Opposition candidate or have him arrested for a criminal offence, but the draftsman of electoral laws has to consider these possibilities. The number of ballot papers in the ballot boxes ought to correspond with the number of ballot papers issued; but if there are not enough it is a simple matter to borrow the perforating machine and stamp some more papers, alter the return of ballot papers issued, and stuff a few more into the ballot boxes. One electoral district is reported to have polled 120 per cent of its electors; but if that is true it was inelegant.

The police, the registration officers, the polling officers, and the counting officers are all public servants whose employees are politicians. For the purposes of the election they may be under the control of an independent Election Commission, but the Commission does not decide promotions and transfers. Even a chief officer of police may have to obey an unlawful order because, if he does not, he may be replaced by a subordinate who does. *Quis custodiet custodes ipsos?* is a pertinent question, and sometimes the answer is a lemon. On the other hand it is not always necessary to break the law. Local officials are such important people that their orders have to be obeyed; and extreme examples are known in which district officers have summoned village headmen in order to indicate to them how the people of their village were to vote.

Candidates for election have admitted that, in their constituencies, none of them has obeyed the law relating to election expenses. It is true that, in such a case, an election can be challenged before an election tribunal. It is, however, an expensive business to challenge elections and sometimes it fails, not because there is no evidence, but because no witnesses are prepared to give it. Why suffer the indignity of standing round in the corridors of the courts for days and days in order to be cross-examined by learned counsel, when one can earn twenty-five rupees by forgetting everything?

Where it is necessary to obey the Ballot Act, politicians in power have other methods of winning elections. Graft and patronage are not peculiar to the States of the United States. Contracts, permits, licences, jobs and so forth have to be given to somebody, and it is unreasonable to expect that they should be awarded to political opponents. Less reprehensible, perhaps, is the use of public expenditure to reward those constituencies which vote the right way, or those portions of constituencies which are deemed to be marginal. The road which was metalled when it passed through the constituency of a Government supporter and unmetalled when it passed through an Opposition constituency was in North America, and I drove along it: but the principle is the same. An Asian Prime Minister who was personally a model of rectitude said that members of the Opposition ought not to be elected because they had failed to obtain schools, clinics, cottage hospitals, roads, and so forth for their constituents.

As I have said already, the picture of electoral corruption produced by these examples is exaggerated. If it were generally true it would be a general indictment of democracy. My listeners in the United Kingdom know that it is not true of British elections. The extent to which it is true elsewhere depends upon local conditions, and I do not suggest that every election in Asia is corrupt, or even that corruption is so general that a genuine exhibition of voters' preferences cannot be obtained. My purpose in raising these issues is twofold. In the first place my examples show that the mere fact that politicians of ability can be found is not a conclusive test for the grant of self-government. The real question is whether the people as a whole is ready for it, and this depends on the general standard of civic responsibility. Secondly, a wide franchise may involve vesting power not in the People with a capital P but in the Politicians with very large Pockets. The politicians who win independence may be, and probably are, men of the utmost probity and public spirit; but their opponents and successors may be rogues like the politician who defeated my friend 'Henry'.

It must be remembered, too, that there are politicians whose appeal to the under-privileged is strong, but whose real purpose is not to establish a social democracy but to supplant it with a dictatorship of which they are to be the instruments. One must not blame the electors; it would be surprising if the homeless population which sleeps in Calcutta's arcades, the slum-dwellers of Bombay, the refugees in Karachi's insanitary colonies, the scheduled castes of Andhra, the boys who throng the approaches to Colombo's railway stations, the porters in the coal-yards, and the landless villagers throughout Asia, were not in favour of bloody revolution. One tends to forget that they are as sensitive and as able as a good, solid English trade-unionist: but the English trade-unionist has won for himself a right to be a person, to hold his job so long as he pulls his weight, to have a house and a garden, to live in conditions which three-quarters of Asia's teeming millions would regard as luxury, to have his children better educated than himself, and to have his family treated when they are sick. There are people richer than he, but they are not much richer, and certainly without cause to be happier. This is an aspect of Britain's homogeneity which I have already stressed, but its importance is seldom realised. In Asia there is greater wealth, more spectacular and more flamboyant, while at the other extreme are hundreds of millions living at a level which Western Europe has long since forgotten and North America never known.

Most of those who capitalise these contrasts and these miseries are not representatives of the people. They do not, as they claim to do, speak for 'the masses'. They are middle-class intellectuals whose social sympathies have out-run their reason, or woolly-minded people whose ambitions have been frustrated by personal deficiencies or a defective home life, or young men in a hurry who got caught up in a movement and cannot get out without thinking themselves to be renegades. Their task is deliberately to subvert the methods of democracy; they delight in outwitting those politicians who try to live on their wits. They use the corrupt methods of the worst party machines with an efficiency greater than that of the party 'boss'. They distribute largesse among their own followers; they provide jobs whenever they can get hold of the patronage; they even give contracts in return for contributions to party funds; they organise strikes wherever they can and whether the strikers are likely to win or lose; they support workers' demands even when (as they sometimes are) they are quite absurd; and they delight in doing these things because their objective is to overthrow the democratic machine. By these methods, too, they obtain a substantial following which is prepared to obey orders; which will, for instance, engage in mass personation at elections, or start a minor riot to discourage other electors from going to the poll, or (if the police are not wary) run off with the ballot boxes. They are quite prepared to make promises which they are unable to keep, because they do not intend to keep them; they can talk the most utter nonsense with impunity, and enjoy it, because they appeal to the illiterate and the downtrodden, the people who have no means of assessing possibilities but who, having nothing to lose, are prepared to listen to any assertion that they have much to gain.

One of the difficulties is to distinguish these *saboteurs* from genuine left-wing movements, designed to effect social reforms by constitutional means and within the limits of the practicable. Left-wing politicians are, as a rule, neither more nor less honest than right-wing politicians. They, too, like power. The communists sometimes support them and sometimes oppose them, according to the prevailing party line, which usually has nothing to do with local conditions. When the communists offer support it is difficult to refuse, for a well-drilled army of supporters, even if small, is a considerable asset; and the local politicians have not had the experience of the Labour Party in the United Kingdom. What is more, during the development of the independence movement the communists infiltrate into nationalist movements, not because they are nationalist but because they are subversive; they seek to make them more revolutionary in the hope that the communists can at a later stage seize power as they seized it in Russia and the rest of Eastern Europe. There were communists in the Indian National Congress and the Ceylon National Congress, though their objectives were soon recognised and they did not obtain even the same measure of success as their fellows in Burma, Indo-China and Indonesia. They are particularly dangerous where the nationalist politicians are themselves corrupt, as in China, because communists are usually not corrupt—they use corrupt methods as the quickest means of destroying constitutional government. Their ultimate objective is not democaracy but domination, the dictatorship of the so-called proletariat, which is in fact the dictatorship of the communist party: but not many of them want to line their own pockets or even to achieve high office.

These are difficult problems, and the constitutional adviser has no ready-made solutions in his folders. Indeed, the main problem is not his concern at all. The point at which these risks can be run with a reasonable chance of success has to be decided at the highest level by those who know the country and its people. In the past, British officials have tended to wait too long; but the nationalist politicians are almost invariably too impatient, and in recent years some of that impatience may have been communicated to the officials. The transition from semi-self-government to independence is a difficult period, and everybody wants to get it over quickly. When it is decided to take action, however, the problem of the franchise must be seriously considered, for it may be possible to minimise the risks by creating a limited franchise or by balancing representation.

If one even calls attention to this sort of problem, one is accused of being 'undemocratic'. Adult franchise is not democratic, however, when it is used corruptly or unconscionably. There are serious risks attached to it, and one must not be frightened by a bad name, though it is equally true that many of those who want to limit the franchise have axes of their own to grind. We are not concerned with countries in which there is something real called 'public opinion'. If there were a Gallup poll in almost any country in Asia or Africa, most of the answers would be 'don't know'. One could get sensible answers to questions about the prospects of the paddy harvest, or whether a school or a clinic was needed in the village, or whether women should be in purdah, or perhaps even whether Kashmir should be Indian or Pakistani: but there would be no sensible answers to most of the questions asked in Delhi, Karachi or Colombo. The notion that a young man from the Law College 'represents' the people because he has been nominated by the Congress, belongs to the majority caste, and speaks the language of the village, is a hypothesis introduced from a country is which opinion is vocal, uniform and (on the whole) founded upon reasonable premises. Much more depends upon the parties than upon the electors, as it used to do in the United States. If the Congress-wallahs from the top to the local committees are good, honest, intelligent patriots, adult franchise will work very well, except perhaps where there are scheduled castes who regard the Congress as the organisation of caste Hindus and the communists as the only people who really believe in—and practise—caste equality. The problem is not peculiar to Asia and Africa. Dickens' description of the election at Eatanswill was only a caricature of a 'democratic' election in a constituency with a wide franchise; and corrupt, machine-made 'politics' was characteristic of many elections in many American States for many years. Indeed, some of those who make fervent speeches about 'democracy' at the meetings of the Trusteeship Council of the United Nations represent countries which have never known an honest election and in which an honest election, if it did occur, would produce astonishing results. It is paradoxical, but true, that in many countries the success of 'democracy' depends upon the character of the oligarchy at the top; the democracy is efficient because the oligarchy is both efficient and honest.

In practice, no doubt, the problems solve themselves. Self-government is usually granted only when the British rulers are satisfied that the oligarchy at the top is honest and patriotic. It is extremely difficult for such an oligarchy to admit that its successors may be corrupt, and so the risk of an adult franchise has usually to be taken. The Commonwealth has had experience of constitutional machinery breaking down. Indeed, since independence the Governments of India and Pakistan have found it necessary to supersede State and Provincial Governments in circumstances which would have been described, ten years ealier, as examples of 'British imperialism'. Fortunately, the powers necessary for the purpose had been inserted in the provisional Constitution framed in 1935, and they were retained in 1947. The notion that everybody will be happy once self-government has been achieved is a delusion fostered by propaganda. Once independence has been granted, however, it is impossible to place such reservations on the power of the oligarchy. If adult franchise is provided for, it is necessary to emphasise that there will be no eggs if all the chickens are eaten, and no chickens if all the eggs are eaten. These facts are well known in the village, but their allegorical importance is not always appreciated.

V

COMMUNALISM IN ELECTIONS

IN my last talk I discussed some of the problems of organising democratic elections in colonial territories. The most difficult question, that of securing adequate communal representation and achieving a balance between competing communal claims, was left for further consideration.

The ultimate objective, of course, is to remove communalism as a political motive, to persuade all the citizens of Arcadia to look at the problems of Arcadia from a national point of view and to ignore all other sentimental interests, whether they are based on race, religion, caste, language or any other social grouping. This does not mean that cultural uniformity must be imposed. Any such suggestion would be strongly resented, particularly in the field of religion. When Indian politicians argue for the secular State they do not want Hindus, Muslims, Buddhists, Christians, Parsees, and so on, to give up their religious beliefs. On the contrary, most of the Indian leaders stress, far more than is done in the West, the importance of religion in personal and national life. What they say is that all religions should be encouraged, but that the State should remain neutral where they are really or apparently in conflict. In other words, a Muslim or a Christian or a Parsee can be as good and as useful a citizen as a Hindu. Nor is it argued that the several languages which people speak, and the literatures expressed in those languages, should not be encouraged. On the contrary, we in Britain encourage and help the Welsh to use and develop their language and literature. What we say is that this is not a political question and that every Member of Parliament, be he English, Welsh, Scots or Irish, or be he Conservative, Labour or Liberal, should regard with favour all steps which enable the Welsh-speaking people to achieve a high cultural standard. In India the problem is more complex but the attitude the same. The many cultures are part of the composite culture of India. Hindi is to become the national language solely for purposes of national government and inter-communication; but the richer the regional languages and literatures become the higher is the standard of Indian civilisation.

Nevertheless, people do think of these things in political terms. Where Christians are in a minority they fear that there will be prejudice against them, that they will not find seats in the legislature or secure posts in the public service, that there will be discrimination in respect of educational establishments, so that Christian schools will not receive adequate grants from public funds, that Christian charities will be hindered or taxed while others are not, and so on. This feeling extends to all minorities. Whereas in undivided India the Hindus objected to communal representation and other forms of communal protection, in Ceylon the Hindus asked for special constitutional protection. The explanation is simple: in India they were a majority, whereas in Ceylon they were a minority.

It is obvious that if in every constituency there are 60 per cent Hindus and 40 per cent Muslims, if in that constituency all the Hindus vote for a single Hindu candidate and all the Muslims vote for a single Muslim candidate, then all the members of the legislature will be Hindus and the Muslims, though 40 per cent of all the electors, will be entirely unrepresented. These hypothetical conditions are never actually attained. Though in some constituencies the Hindus will be in a majority, in others the Muslims will be in a majority. Also, the majority vote is quite likely to be split among two or more candidates. The minority vote may also be split, but that is less likely because, unless the majority vote is split, a Muslim has little chance of being elected. Further, even where communal feelings are strong, it is not true that everybody votes communally. In undivided India the National Congress, though primarily Hindu, always claimed to be nationalist and non-communal, and it always contained some Muslims, Christians and others. The communal organisation, the Hindu Mahasabha, was a much less powerful organisation. At the other extreme the Communist Party and the various non-communist socialist parties have been non-communal, though as a matter of tactics they almost invariably take care to put up candidates of the right community in the right constituency: that is, they assume that communist voters have communal prejudices.

The difficulty of communal representation is that it encourages the defect that it seeks to remedy. If a constituency is specifically designated as Muslim or Christian, the member elected for it is primarily a Muslim or a Christian, and only secondarily a conservative, a liberal or a socialist. In the legislature he is expected to act primarily in defence of Muslim or Christian interests; and, if he does not, he may lose his seat next time to a person who is considered to be more active in defence of Muslim or Christian interests. There can be little doubt that communal representation in India before 1947 and in Ceylon before 1931 encouraged communalism.

If possible, therefore, one should avoid communal electorates, though it is often politically necessary to have them. They existed in Ceylon before 1931, but were then replaced by ordinary territorial constituencies with straight voting. This system undoubtedly operated to the disadvantage of the minorities. Before 1931 they were over-represented; after 1931 they were under-represented. In consequence there grew up a demand for 'fifty-fifty'—in other words that steps be taken to ensure that the number of minority members was equal to the number of Sinhalese members. This would have given the minorities over-representation, since the Sinhalese are about two-thirds of the population and more than two-thirds of the electors. It was argued, however, that only by 'balanced representation' was it possible to ensure that the Sinhalese would not combine against the minorities.

The Sinhalese would not accept any such arrangement; and when in 1943 the Ministers were asked to draft a constitutional scheme, they decided to aim at a system of representation which neither over-represented nor under-represented the Sinhalese. One fact which helped towards a solution, and which incidentally shows the value of the local knowledge which Jeremy Bentham did not possess of Mexico, was that the minorities were strongest in the more sparsely populated provinces. If, therefore, the provinces were weighted for area as well as for population, a reasonably proportionate representation could be given. There were, too, other advantages of this arrangement. Among the Sinhalese it weighted the more backward Kandyan areas against the more prosperous low-country areas, and it weighted the rural areas against the densely-populated West Coast, which had always played a disproportionate part in Ceylon politics. It was of course not a disadvantage that the rural areas were more likely than the West Coast to support the party which the Ministers intended to form. To make certain that any substantial portion of electors belonging to a racial, religious or caste minority was given representation, the Delimitation Commission was authorised to increase or diminish the size of a constituency in order to take account of 'community or diversity of interest'.

This arrangement was approved by the Soulbury Commission and the United Kingdom Government and has worked quite well for two general elections. It was said by its critics that it gave representation to the elephants and the fishes—in other words the more jungle and the more lagoons the higher the representation. The reason for basing weightage on area was, however, that it distributed twenty-five seats according to a principle. If it had been decided to distribute twenty-five seats to help the minorities there would have been persistent haggling. Obviously this arrangement depended on local conditions, but the principle of applying weightage to help minorities may be applicable elsewhere.

It is in fact very rare to have a strict application of the rule 'one vote, one value'. We have seen that even in homogeneous Britain the rural areas of Wales and Scotland are given increased representation so as to avoid very large constituencies in respect of area. Also, it is still thought necessary to represent communities in the English sense—counties and boroughs—in order to get some corporate spirit into a constituency or group of constituencies. Counties are split, and counties are combined, but county boundaries are not crossed. Elsewhere in the Commonwealth rural interests are often balanced against urban interests. In South Africa the two phrases, 'community or diversity of interests' and 'sparsity or density of population' both appear in the Constitution, though the variations from the norm must not exceed 15 per cent either way. Generally this has been used to weight the rural areas at the expense of the urban areas, and this almost automatically favours the Afrikaners at the expense of the English-speaking people.

This system of weightage lends itself to jerrymandering, which has indeed been alleged both in Australia and in South Africa. It is not easy to provide an impartial Delimitation Commission because, unless the Commission is given a clear directive, the decision whether to weight or not to weight must be a matter of policy. This is particularly true where there is no limit on the variation, as in Ceylon. In South Africa there is a limit of 15 per cent, but it has been said in evidence that the Commissions have varied considerably in the degree to which the weighting factors have been taken into consideration.

The listener may have wondered why the Ceylonese Ministers went to the trouble of enfranchising elephants and fishes when a system of proportional representation would have achieved the same result. The simple answer is that proportional representation requires the voter to mark his preferences on a ballot paper, and this cannot be done by an illiterate person. Actually the draft scheme for an elected Senate, or Second Chamber, which was never approved by the Ministers because they decided to leave the question to the first Parliament, did provide for the proportional representation of Provinces by means of the single transferable vote. It was realised that this would disfranchise the illiterate; but it was thought not to be objectionable to do so for a Second Chamber whose powers would be narrowly limited.

There are other objections to proportional representation, especially in a plural society. Wherever it exists it encourages the development of small parties, which in turn produce a series of coalition Governments. Such

Governments are almost always unstable, and they depend more on secret negotiations by party leaders than on a choice by the electorate. England, said Disraeli, does not love coalitions: nor does any other country, for they encourage intrigue and backstair politics. Ceylon itself exhibits the danger: for though the United National Party and its allies have held a majority since 1947, there is no alternative Government possible except a coalition of splinter parties. If proportional representation could be adopted, it would probably split the United National Party into fragments. What is more, in a plural society the encouragement of splinter parties necessarily means the encouragement of communal parties.

Ceylon has, however, a primitive form of proportional representation in its multi-member constituencies. The idea was suggested by the Soulbury Commission as a means for securing the representation of communally mixed areas. The best example is to be found in the most cosmopolitan constituency in Ceylon, Colombo Central. It contains European, Indian and Pakistani residents as well as most types of Ceylonese—Sinhalese, Tamils, Moors, Burghers and Malays, Buddhists, Hindus, Muslims and Christians. It is impossible to sort them out into separate constituencies, and so it has been made into a three-member constituency. The illiterate voters cannot be expected to mark an order of preferences, and so each voter is given three ballot papers, which he may mark as he pleases. That is, he may give three votes to one candidate, or two votes to one and his third vote to a second, or one vote to each of three candidates. The idea was that a minority group would concentrate its votes, while a majority group would tend to disperse them.

Exactly what has happened it is impossible to say,

but the results have been unexpected. At both elections a communist was elected, though he belonged to the smallest racial group, the Burghers. In 1947 the United National Party secured two seats, one a Sinhalese and one a Muslim. In 1952 they secured only one seat, that of the Muslim, while the third seat went to a Muslim who generally supports the United National Party, though he stood in opposition to the party. Thus the two largest racial groups, the Sinhalese and the Tamils, the Buddhists and the Hindus, are completely unrepresented. Possibly the explanation is that sophisticated Colombo thinks more in terms of party than in terms of community: and this may be because elsewhere communal representation has been avoided. The multi-member constituency favours communal voting; but generally speaking the temptation seems to have been avoided, at least in Colombo.

If communal representation has to be adopted, it may take several forms. The logical form, which the first Constituent Assembly suggested for Pakistan, is to divide the electorate according to community and to have separate constituencies and separate registers for each community. For instance, if in the Province of Arcadia the Muslims are entitled to seven seats, the caste Hindus to two seats, and the scheduled castes to one seat, all the scheduled castes of the Province form a single constituency; for the election of caste Hindus the Province has to be divided into two constituencies, each with a register containing the names of caste Hindus only; finally, for the election of Muslims, the Province has to be divided into seven constituencies, each with a purely Muslim register. Separate polling stations have then to be provided wherever there is a sufficient concentration of Muslims, caste Hindus or scheduled castes, as the case may be.

This system accepts the logic of communal representation and, in large measure, takes the communal problem out of politics. On the one hand a Muslim candidate does not have to appeal for Hindu votes; on the other hand he does not have to appeal to the communal sentiments of the Muslims in order to keep out a Hindu or a pro-Hindu. The advantages and disadvantages of this method cannot be determined in general terms, for they depend upon local conditions. It is clear, however, that it accepts the 'two-nation' theory as being a permanent feature of the country. It does not pretend that the two nations will in due course be welded into one people. At best it assumes a partnership.

The system adopted in undivided India was rather more complicated. There were separate electoral registers for Sikhs, Muslims, Anglo-Indians, Europeans and Indian Christians: but there were no separate registers for Hindus, because all seats which were not specifically allocated were called 'general seats', and anybody who was not on a special electoral register could be an elector for a general seat. Since these general seats were almost invariably held by Hindus, the system was much the same as that already described: but it had this difference, that certain of the general seats were reserved for scheduled castes and, in Bombay, for Marathas. If a general seat was reserved for a member of a scheduled caste, all the electors had the right to vote, without respect of caste, but the candidates had to be members of the scheduled castes.

This idea is obviously capable of extension. In the hypothetical case of the Province of Arcadia, it would be possible to divide the Province into ten constituencies only, to make no distinction of race or caste on the registers of those constituencies, but to designate two constituencies for caste Hindu members and one for a member from the scheduled castes. One would thus have Hindus voting for Muslims, Muslims voting for Hindus, and members of all castes voting for the higher castes and the scheduled castes. Whether such a scheme would work would depend on the intensity of racial, religious and caste feeling.

The Hindus who dominated the Indian National Congress objected entirely to communal representation, though they were willing to go some way to compromise with the Muslim League, which insisted on it. The Hindus of India, like the Sinhalese in Ceylon, were quite sincere in their opposition: they wanted to create a national State in which religion was irrelevant for political or secular purposes. Indeed they alleged that communal feeling was created, or at least stimulated, by the British in order to cause Indians to disagree and thus to postpone the transfer of power. On an impartial view of history I do not think such an interpretation tenable. There were actions by the Government of India which may have accentuated communal feeling. After the Mutiny there was considerable suspicion of the Muslims; later on emphasis was given to the so-called 'martial races', many of which were Muslims in the recruitment of the Indian Army; and there was much antagonism to the Congress-wallahs, as they were called, when the Congress became more virulent against British rule and especially when Mahatma Gandhi's specific of non-violent non-co-operation was adopted.

The migrations and massacres which followed the separation of India and Pakistan in 1947 showed how strong was communal feeling, and they were apparently unexpected both by the Hindus and by the Muslims. Nevertheless, the experience of the Government of the United Kingdom in trying to find solutions for the communal problem shows not only how difficult it can be, but also that its own *bona fides* is quite likely to be attacked.

The Congress solution was not communal representation but a Bill of Rights guaranteeing those rights which the minority communities might suspect to be in jeopardy. I must discuss this question separately in my next talk, for it raises wider issues than communal issues. It may be noted, however, that in the present Constitution of India special provision, of a temporary nature, is included for the scheduled castes and the Anglo-Indians. The first Constituent Assembly of Pakistan, on the other hand, proposed a Bill of Rights as well as communal representation. The Indian gesture gives an indication of one approach to the problem. The minorities demand special representation because they fear discrimination. It may be possible to meet those fears by some different means. The Anglo-Indians were specially concerned with employment in certain public services in which they had preference. That preference has been temporarily preserved but will gradually disappear. A similar problem arose in Ceylon. The Tamils had been able to secure, by open competition, a higher proportion of public appointments than the Sinhalese. They feared that, with a Sinhalese majority, there would be danger of discrimination. Hence all appointments and promotions in the public service are placed under the control of an independent Public Service Commission. Another problem often raised is that of financial assistance to schools. Various groups, especially minority groups, often fear discrimination. The draft Constitution for Pakistan, among others, contained an article intended to prevent such discrimination. It will be seen that the solution may be not to provide special representation in the legislature but to ask what special dangers there are, and to try to meet those dangers by specific constitutional provisions.

The experience of the Asian countries of the Commonwealth shows once more how important it is for Jeremy Bentham to go to Mexico if he proposes to prescribe for Mexico. Modesty compels me to assume that the same principle applies to anybody in Asia pretending to prescribe for Africa. Nevertheless, the communal problem is too important to be passed over in silence. Where it is a problem among the Africans themselves and arises through religious differences, language differentiation, or tribal loyalties, the lesson to be learned from Asia is that study on the spot may produce an acceptable solution. The fundamental problem in some parts of Africa, however, is that the Europeans, the Indians and the Africans are economically important in inverse proportion to their numbers. It would probably be agreed, too, that the assistance of each group is essential for the effective government of the country. What the solution is, or ought to be, cannot be determined from a distance, nor decided upon general principles. It would seem, however, that communal segregation is economically impracticable, because the revenues produced by the Europeans and the Indians must be used for the benefit of the Africans.

It would seem, too, that to integrate Europeans, Indians and Africans into one nation is at present impracticable. Socially they are almost completely segregated. Nor is this only a question of racial prejudice. Indians always tend to segregate themselves wherever they are—even in Ceylon and Burma—because of their peculiar social system. They regard themselves as Indians even after several generations. They do not, and under their social conventions cannot, marry outside their communities. After two thousand years, more or less, the Tamils of Ceylon are still socially segregated from the Sinhalese though they no longer regard themselves as Indians and share a common national loyalty with the Sinhalese.

Communal representation, as I have said, encourages communalism; and what a self-governing country must develop is not communalism but common loyalty. Even so, the first step towards common loyalty is inter-communal co-operation; and to develop that co-operation it is necessary to recognize communal distinctions and to enable each community to play its part in national development. At this stage of affairs it is impossible to hope for integration, but partnership is not impossible. Nor is there any reason to fear lack of co-operation once a definite constitutional status is assured. The Indians remain Indians, but they are always anxious, as they are in Ceylon and Pakistan, to be regarded as citizens of their adopted country and to take part in its political life. The so-called Europeans ought rather to be thought of as citizens of the United Kingdom, for they have special characteristics which are not necessarily common to all Europeans. One of those characteristics is a capacity to adapt themselves to new conditions. Since independence came to India, Pakistan, Ceylon and Burma the Europeans there have behaved with quite remarkable discretion. They fear for their property and their jobs: but if the Constitution is so devised that these are protected, all the precedents suggest that they will collaborate wholeheartedly in the development of the country.

VI

A BILL OF RIGHTS

THE idea of a Bill of Rights incorporated in the Constitution derives from the first country to leave what is now called the Commonwealth—the United States of America. Having experienced what they regarded or at least proclaimed as the tyranny of George III and his Parliaments, several of the States had included in their Constitutions limitations on the powers of their Governments and legislatures, designed to ensure the liberties which they had learned to prize as British subjects but which could, as they had learned, be taken away by legislation. When the Constitution of the United States was referred to the States for their ratification, several of them expressed apprehension that it contained no provision limiting the legislative power of the Congress. Accordingly, the first Congress passed a resolution in September 1789, submitting twelve amendments to the States. Ten of these were accepted and make up the Bill of Rights.

The rights so protected derive from the experience of England in the eighteenth century. They include religious freedom, the right of assembly, the right to petition, the right to carry arms, the restriction of billeting, freedom from searches and seizures, indictment by grand jury, the rule that a person cannot be charged twice for the same offence, or be forced to be a witness against himself, or be deprived of his life, liberty or property without due process of law, and so on. There was nothing in the Bill of Rights against racial or religious discrimination. The problem had not arisen in

1789, and in any case the Bill of Rights was a series of limitations on the United States, while discrimination would be primarily a matter for the individual States. The provisions against discrimination are to be found in the 14th and 15th amendments, enacted after the Civil War. President Lincoln had purported by proclamation to free the slaves in the Southern States; and after the North had won, the 13th amendment was passed to abolish slavery throughout the United States. The 14th amendment was designed to give citizenship to all persons born or naturalised in the United States and to protect the rights and immunities of all citizens even against the States. The 15th amendment forbade the curtailment of the right to vote on the ground of race, religion or previous condition of servitude.

These provisions do not in themselves provide any precedent for other colonies which achieve independence. The first ten amendments relate to conditions in the United States in 1789. The 13th, 14th and 15th amendments deal with the consequences of slavery, which had long since been abolished in those territories which remained part of the British Empire. Indeed in England slavery had been declared illegal by a decision of Lord Mansfield in 1771. It is generally agreed, too, that the essential political and personal freedoms are even better protected in the United Kingdom than they are in the United States, in spite of the fact that there are no constitutional limitations on the powers of the Parliament of the United Kingdom.

It is sometimes alleged by nationalist politicians struggling for the freedom of their country, and still more often by communist agitators, that British practice in the colonies differs from that in the United Kingdom. Without studying in detail the laws of all the colonies, it would be impossible for me to assert dogmatically that

British practice has always followed the best constitutional principles. To anyone who has seen colonial government at work, however, it is quite remarkable how British officials carry into their own administration the principles that they have learned at home. It is easy enough for officials in the United Kingdom to behave tolerantly and justly; and if they become too zealous in the prosecution of the Government's objectives there is always a Parliament to recall them to the strait path of constitutional government. It is not so easy in a colony moving towards freedom, where the officials are publicly denounced as agents of imperialism, exploiters of the local people, toadies of the Governor, arrogant exponents of colour prejudice, and every other epithet which frustrated nationalism or personal or political ambition can invent. The fact that these epithets can be used openly and without penal consequences is in itself proof that constitutional principles are observed. It is only when abuse goes beyond abuse and becomes incitement to disorder that action is taken.

Even more important is the fact that nationalist politics and public opinion generally become imbued with these same constitutional principles. I mentioned in my first talk that the British people had been remarkably successful in propagating the concepts of British justice. The lessons that have been learned and taught in the Inns of Court and Westminster Hall have spread around the world and are illustrated every day by arguments at the Bar, pronouncements from the Bench, and speeches in the legislature. Accordingly, the presumption is that the constitutional guarantee of principles of civil and political liberty is unnecessary.

It may be urged that, since everybody agrees with these constitutional principles, there is no harm in them. My answer is that there can be a great deal of potential harm in any formulation of constitutional guarantees. No draftsman can produce a formula which will be satisfactory even in the short run, and I speak as one who has tried. In the Constitution of Ceylon there is one provision against discrimination. It is not exactly as I drafted it, and I twice tried to get it amended before it was made law. Had my draft been approved there would have been less argument about it later on. It is nevertheless true that a court of first instance declared invalid a piece of legislation which was never intended to be covered by the provision, and it was necessary to go to the Privy Council before it could be definitely ascertained that the legislation was within the power of the Parliament of Ceylon.

This is by no means an unusual experience. The constitutional guarantees in the Constitution of the United States have often been used by vested interests to obstruct legislation which was clearly desired by the people of the United States and which did not affect any constitutional principles as we in Britain would understand them. President F. D. Roosevelt's 'New Deal' was so obstructed until, in course of time, more liberal judges replaced the conservative judges on the Supreme Court of the United States. The Constitution of India contains a most careful formulation of constitutional guarantees. Almost before the ink was dry difficulties were discovered. One major aspect of Congress policy, the abolition of the *zamindari* or landlord system was found to be forbidden by the Constitution. The unusual step had to be taken of validating by constitutional amendment no less than thirteen legislative Acts. The formulation of fundamental rights accepted by the first Constituent Assembly of Pakistan forbade certain types of legislation which have been in operation in Britain, with the approval of all parties, for seventy-five years. Such legislation had not been enacted in India or Pakistan and therefore it was not realized that the phrasing of the constitutional guarantees was rendering it invalid.

The constitutional expert ought to know something of the social and economic problems of the country with which he is dealing, but he cannot be expected to be omniscient. In any case he has not the gift of prophecy and therefore he does not know what social and economic problems are likely to be raised in future, or what legislative devices may be needed to solve them. In formulating constitutional restrictions designed to prevent abuses which experience has shown to be possible, he may and probably will forbid methods of preventing abuses likely to arise in the future. Constitutions last for centuries. In 1789 nobody could have foreseen that the United States would become a great nation of 150 million people inhabiting the greater part of a continent, that it would have a vast capitalist organisation which enabled this great population to maintain a high standard of living through the use of electricity and the internal combustion engine, that the normal method of communication would be by air, and that atomic energy promised an almost unlimited supply of power. Nevertheless, the Constitution of the United States is in all essentials as it was drafted in 1789.

It is true that the Constitution of the United States has been adapted by the interpretation of generations of great judges. Nevertheless, if the constitutional lawyers of the United States were at liberty to prepare a new draft not very much would be left of the old one. The less one puts into a Constitution the better, and in particular the fewer restrictions there are on legislation the more likely it will be that successive generations of legislators will be able to solve the country's political problems.

This principle must not be carried too far. The

British Constitution, for all practical purposes, contains one clause: 'There shall be a Parliament, and it may do what it pleases.' But we are a conservative people, and Parliament is truly British, for it makes changes cautiously. Most of the world has become republican; but we have kept our monarchy, and now we pride ourselves on being so sensible. We do not need to defend the monarchy any longer, for it does its job better than any institution that the lawyer could devise. We have carefully preserved the independence of our judges, and we do not require a constitutional provision to protect them. Free elections and the political liberties needed for party controversy are part of our tradition and need not be specifically embodied in the laws. We do not fear a communist *coup d'état* or a fascist revolution, for no communist or fascist ever gets enough support to be more than a nuisance. We have no laws against discrimination because our laws do not discriminate—though they did so in the past when there was thought to be a connection between religion and treason.

This conservative tradition is the product of centuries of experience. We can share our experience with the colonies, but we cannot guarantee that colonies which had no such experience will necessarily acquire the sort of intuition which enables us to react almost by instinct against interference with fundamental liberties. It may therefore be desirable to prevent the new legislature from passing some kinds of legislation which the Parliament of the United Kingdom could enact. Once more I cannot be dogmatic, for much depends on local conditions. Here, however, we are in the realm of general principles.

In the first place, the main constitutional structure must be protected. No Constitution can protect a country against revolution, but a revolution is rarely to be feared. The modern technique is for a small revolutionary junta to ally itself with democratic parties, to get key institutions like the army, the police and the radio into its hands, and then to push out its allies or blackguard them into becoming subservient hangers-on. There is, however, another technique, which is being used in Burma, Malaya, Indonesia and East Africa, that of creating a resistance movement which seeks to disrupt normal economic life, to overawe sections of the population by threats of violence, and generally to make the machinery of government run down. This has to be met by exactly the opposite of constitutional guarantees, for the Government must be entrusted with wide discretionary powers of an emergency character. Possibly the Americans are so hysterical about their handful of communists, because they realise that they cannot in accordance with the rules of their Constitution handle a movement for widespread resistance to lawful authority. The Constitution assumes that the people of the United States are good, solid law-abiding citizens who are completely trustworthy until they become politicians.

The protection of the main constitutional structure is not an easy matter, because there is no reason why the details should remain static. For instance, it is unnecessary to prescribe for all time the qualifications and disqualifications of members of Parliament, nor the oaths that they should take, nor the emoluments that they should receive. One wants to make certain that it is a democratic Parliament, but not that it has all the characteristics that are thought desirable in 1956. Nor, again, is it necessary to give constitutional protection to the monarchy. The Constitution of India works almost as well—perhaps for the time being it works just as well—as it would if Dr Rajendra Prasad were a Governor-General appointed by the Queen. There is no reason why Ceylon should not become a republic if a future generation so desires, and equally no reason why India should not restore the monarchy if it finds itself saddled with a series of undesirable Presidents.

The general tendency is to put too much into the Constitution. India has produced an enormous document of 268 printed pages. The official index of its provisions runs to fifty-two printed pages. The text is not as long as the Government of India Act, 1935, which ran to 324 pages. That Act applied also to Pakistan, but it has been cut down by legislation since 1947 to 111 pages. India and Pakistan are very complex countries, and detailed regulation is essential: but not the whole of it needs to be constitutionally protected.

The best way to protect democracy is to ensure democratic election. This involves, as in India, an autonomous Election Commission charged with responsibility for delimiting constituencies, compiling electoral registers, and running elections. This in itself is not enough, for elections are not free if the minions of a Hitler or a Stalin are allowed to decide who shall be candidates. On the other hand, it is not at all easy to draft appropriate constitutional provisions to guarantee free elections. Those of us who have adopted British traditions tend to think in terms of the fundamental political liberties, freedom of speech, freedom of assembly and freedom of association. On the other hand, we in Britain have never accepted the theory that politicians can advocate treason or sedition or, what comes to the same thing, a policy of advocating the overthrow of constitutional government by force or fraud. As the law now stands, and as it has stood for a couple of centuries, any revolutionary party is a seditious conspiracy.

We do not need to protect the Constitution against fascists and communists because they are too unimportant in Britain. *De minimis non curat lex.* That is not so in all the countries of the Commonwealth and, if it be true that a political party advocates the overthrow of the Constitution as by law established, there is nothing in the principles of democracy which requires that it be tolerated. For many years a Roman Catholic could not be elected to Parliament because the activities of the Papacy, and particularly the excommunication of Elizabeth I, led people to believe that the Roman Catholic Church was a conspiracy against the English Constitution. Whether they were right or wrong is not my concern: all I am saying is that democracy does not require us to give legal protection to those who seek to overthrow democracy. So far as I know, nobody has tried to draft appropriate provisions, and I am sure it would not be easy to do so. Nevertheless, it seems better to protect democracy in that way than to lay down constitutional guarantees of political liberties which can be used to protect anti-democratic forces as well as democratic forces. India has already met the difficulty and has had to amend its Constitution *ex post facto*.

Another institution which needs to be protected is the judiciary. An independent judiciary is fundamental to 'British justice' and everybody agrees with the principle. Such protection is given in England by requiring that a judge hold his commission during good behaviour but be removable after resolution of both Houses of Parliament. That provision is ambiguous and is amended in most Dominion Constitutions. It is also provided that the salaries of superior judges shall be charged on the Consolidated Fund and not voted annually—a provision which is supported by the parliamentary practice requiring that criticism of a judge be on a substantive motion.

There is a tendency to carry these constitutional

provisions too far and to include in the Constitution too many detailed provisions relating to the judiciary. The Indian Constitution is notorious in this respect, and it has been said, with conscious exaggeration, that an Indian judge cannot blow his nose without express constitutional authority. In Pakistan there was a suggestion again as a joke, for a constitutional provision that all judges' chairs have cushions in order that they might sit fairly and freely, without favour and without fear. There is an explanation for this strange anxiety to lay down the details of the judicial establishment for all time. There is a genuine fear of political influence upon the judiciary.

This problem cannot be solved by the constitutional lawyer, for the independence and impartiality of the judiciary are not secured by constitutional provisions. These qualities are derived from the independence and probity of the Bar. For those who are not very familiar with British justice in its homeland, emphasis must be placed upon the probity as well as on the independence of the Bar. Lawyers generally have not a good reputation because in the scramble for fees they are not always careful of the interests of their clients. It is not very easy for that sort of lawyer to become an impartial and incorruptible judge, for his sense of moral rectitude must have become perverted. The professional public opinion which persists in the Inns of Court is therefore very important. It is easy to make a joke over a glass of port which makes the listener feel uncomfortable even though he has to treat it as a joke. If he has any sort of conscience, he will take care not to be the subject of such jokes again.

Institutions like the Inns of Court do not exist in the colonies, but some of them have Law Libraries which are not merely libraries but common rooms in which barristers chat to each other while waiting for their cases to be called and, incidentally, waiting for solicitors to hand over their well-marked briefs. The public opinion developed in that way is, I think, more important than constitutional provisions. Such provisions are necessary; but it is important not to ossify the legal system by inserting too much detail. The system of administration of justice handed over by the British is not the height of perfection. In the course of fifty or a hundred years changes will be necessary to meet the developing genius of the people. It must be emphasised again that the constitutional draftsman has not the gift of prophecy. The more modest he is, the less he seeks to bind future generations, the more successful he is likely to be.

It will be noticed that I have barely touched upon one problem with which this talk ought to be much concerned, that of using a Bill of Rights to prevent discrimination in respect of race, religion and caste. One explanation is that such provisions are rarely successful. There is still more racial discrimination in the United States, in spite of the 14th and 15th amendments, than there is in the United Kingdom. Laws cannot be effective if they go far beyond public opinion, and it is only recently that American opinion has shown any anxiety to give effect to the amendments in the spirit as well as in the letter. It is significant that the Supreme Court has now begun to reconsider the decisions under which real discrimination was allowed under the shadow of conformity with formal law.

India has gone to great trouble to try to prevent discrimination by constitutional guarantees, partly because before 1947 the Congress was very insistent that the conflict between Hindu and Muslim, on which the British rulers laid such stress, could be resolved by a Bill of

Rights. So far as religious discrimination is concerned, the provisions are likely to be successful. Hinduism is a tolerant religion, though like every other religion it can become intolerant if it is hitched to politics. In the neighbouring country of Ceylon there are people known as political Buddhists. Buddhism is as tolerant as Hinduism, but Buddhist sentiment is so strong among sections of the electorate that some politicians have found it politically convenient to arouse sentiments which seem to be distinctly unBuddhist. This is made easier by the fact that Christianity is strong among the wealthier classes, so that political Buddhism has some of the characteristics of a class war.

The situation might have been the same in India had it remained undivided. There the opponent would have been not Christianity but Islam; and Islam is powerful because it dominates the Muslim's life. The conflicts among the Muslim sects can be quite fierce, as they have been recently in Pakistan, and the political divisions among Muslims can be acute. Nor is Islam the aggressive religion that it was seven hundred years ago. Nevertheless, the Muslim League showed that the brotherhood of Islam is very real; and the great fast of Ramazan is such a test of fortitude that it helps to cement the bonds of those who subject themselves to it. This problem, I believe, has disappeared in India because the Muslims are now a small minority, whose political influence is too small to justify a departure from the principles of toleration which the Congress genuinely upholds.

India seems likely to be much less successful in its attempt to avoid discrimination according to caste. This problem is not likely to arise outside the Asian countries of the Commonwealth, but it illustrates the principle that one cannot change deeply imbedded social ideas by constitutional guarantees. It has been said that one cannot make people good by Act of Parliament. It should be added that one cannot overthrow a social system by drafting a Constitution. There seems to be no real change in the attitude of the caste Hindus to the scheduled castes, in spite of the striking example of Mr Nehru's own family. Nor is the conflict between Brahmin and non-Brahmin less acute than it was in 1947.

The conclusion to be drawn from the experience of India, Pakistan and Ceylon is, I think, that one should not attempt to deal with the problem of minorities by constitutional guarantees in Bills of Rights. One should try to find out where the shoe is likely to pinch and to provide the necessary flexibility at that point.

It must nevertheless be remembered that a Constitution ought to be acceptable to the great mass of the people. A proposal should never be rejected on purely theoretical grounds. If there is a real demand for constitutional guarantees they ought to be inserted, and the task of the draftsman should be to make them as flexible as possible. This may compel the use of vague phrases like 'reasonable' and 'in the public interest'. The Courts of Law are not really competent to decide whether legislation is 'reasonable' and 'in the public interest', but if there is no alternative they may be called upon to do so. What the draftsman has to do is to provide a Constitution which will work; and it will work if it is acceptable to public opinion. Like the civil servant who said, 'If you must do this silly thing why must you do it in this silly way' he must say 'If you must have a Bill of Rights let it be as flexible as possible'.

VII

THE LEGISLATURE

THE old problem of the need for a Second Chamber is seldom argued nowadays. Just as, in Britain, the Labour Party has come round to the view that the House of Lords, with its present restricted powers, does little harm and some good, so in the rest of the Commonwealth opinion is almost unanimous that some kind of Second Chamber is required. For this attitude, there are several reasons.

First, the larger plural societies must have federal Constitutions in order to maintain unity in diversity, or more properly diversity in unity. The general principle adopted in the United States is then generally followed. The First Chamber represents the people of the federation; the Second Chamber represents the several units—States or Provinces. By varying the composition of the Second Chamber and weighting the powers of the two Chambers, it is possible to achieve a communal balance. In this respect the experience of Pakistan is particularly instructive. There the units vary greatly in size and importance. East Bengal has a population of forty-six millions, as large as that of England and Wales. West Pakistan, which is a thousand miles away, has a population of thirty-seven million: but that population was divided among five Provinces, six States which had acceded to Pakistan, and a group of States combined in the Baluchistan States Union. For nearly seven years progress in Constitution-making was hindered by the difficulty of achieving a balance between East and West Pakistan. Mr Muhammad Ali, the late Prime Minister, then evolved a complicated formula involving joint sittings of the two Chambers and specific minorities from both sections. It was a very complicated arrangement, for it implied that the Government could not be responsible to the first House, in which East Pakistan was to have a majority, nor to the second House, in which West Pakistan was to have a majority, but only to a joint sitting in which they were equally represented. It was by no means easy to draft these provisions; and when they were drafted there were grave doubts whether they were workable.

There was no doubt that the principle of parity between East and West had to be adopted, but it seemed better to make West Pakistan a unit, as East Pakistan already was, and to have only one Chamber in which they would be equally represented. This involved the fusion of the Provinces and States of West Pakistan into a single Province. There were other reasons for this suggestion, and they were in fact the conclusive reasons. Communal rivalry among the Punjabis, the Sindhis, the Pathans, the Baluchis, and so forth, was said to be exaggerated by having separate Governments consisting of ambitious politicians competing with each other and sometimes with the federal politicians. Historically and economically, West Pakistan was said to be a unit, which had been broken up by British rule. Unity was said to be the tradition of Islam, though with East Pakistan separated from West Pakistan by a thousand miles of Indian territory it was impracticable to convert Pakistan into a unitary State. There was of course a risk that rivalry between East and West would become more acute where they confronted each other in a single legislature, but it was assumed that party lines would cut across the Provincial boundaries, and that both East and West would be represented in the Federal Government.

Secondly, even where a unitary Constitution is involved, the second Chamber may produce a different communal balance from the first. Thus in South Africa the House of Assembly represented the population of the Union, while the Senate was designed to represent the Provinces. Since two of the Provinces had an Afrikaner majority and two had an English majority, the balance was important: but it has now been destroyed by recent legislation designed to give the Nationalist Government a two-thirds majority at a joint sitting, so that the Constitution can be amended without the support of the Opposition.

Usually the principle applied in the First Chamber has to be what in the conflicts of the old Province of Canada was called 'Rep. by Pop.', or representation according to population. In the Second Chamber equality of representation is more easily accorded. The problem then is to achieve a balance of power between First Chamber and Second Chamber.

Thirdly, politics in many parts of the Commonwealth overseas involves a fiercer conflict than it does in the United Kingdom, and many persons of eminence and ability are reluctant to take part in it. This may be so even where there are no communal differences, as in Australia. The bitterness of Irish politics seems to have been carried to Australia and to have taken root there. Where there is communal diversity, however, there may be even greater bitterness at elections because few candidates can resist appealing to the racial, religious and other prejudices of the electors.

Indeed it is everywhere true that the ablest persons in the country do not take an active part in politics. This can be seen in the House of Commons, where few persons of outstanding ability are to be found. The ablest of each generation go into the universities, the professions, the public service and business. They become full-time salaried employees and cannot find the time for nursing constituencies or attending lengthy debates. This is no criticism of the House of Commons. There may be difficulty in finding suitable Ministers, but in principle the House ought to consist not of unusual, extraordinary or eccentric people, but of people who share the ideas and prejudices of the ordinary electors.

In less well-developed countries there may even be difficulty in securing persons of suitable quality to act as representatives. The distances which they have to travel are usually greater, so that politics becomes a full-time occupation. In London many Members follow their careers and attend the House when their day's work is done. Such an arrangement is rarely possible in Ottawa, Canberra, Pretoria, New Delhi or Karachi. The number of people who can afford to enter upon the insecure job of professional politician is obviously limited.

Ceylon has a characteristic which it shares with many colonies, the enormous attraction of the public service. It is not an exaggeration to say that every parent in the Island hopes that his son will enter that service, whether the job to which he thinks he can aspire is that of Permanent Secretary or that of peon. Even the medical profession is almost entirely staffed by public servants. Only the law, which is a jealous mistress, and rarely favours those who spend time on politics, is independent of Government control. Business is in a large measure in the hands of Europeans and Indians. Ceylon has a population of eight millions, and its standard of living is higher than in most tropical colonies. Nevertheless, the section of the population which can be expected to take an active interest in politics is small. The public service takes an enormous chunk out of that section, and it is usually the abler chunk. Hence it is by no means easy to maintain the quality of the House of Representatives.

The Second Chamber helps to solve these various problems. Nobody would defend the composition of the House of Lords as it is at present: it remains unaltered only because agreement cannot be reached on proposals for reform. It has, however, one admirable feature. Cabinet Ministers and experienced politicians of all parties are given peerages on their retirement from active politics. The ablest lawyers are to be found there because they help in the judicial work of the House, though (apart from the Lord Chancellor and his predecessors) they do not engage in controversial debates. The ablest diplomats, civil servants, officers from the services, medical practitioners, business men, and so on, are given peerages. The level of ability among peers of the first generation is therefore high. It is true, as has often been pointed out, that a person who achieves professional success is not necessarily the sort of person who can handle the generalities of politics; but it is also true that on many matters of a less controversial character which come before Parliament the opinions expressed in the House of Lords are more cogent than those expressed in the House of Commons. It cannot be argued that the peers of the first generation, or indeed of any generation, ought to override the wishes of the people as expressed in the House of Commons. It is, however, a fallacy to assume that the essential function of Parliament is to settle controversial issues. These secure the publicity, but a great deal of the work is comparatively technical; and in that part a person who has the administrator's attitude of mind may be more useful than a great orator or an astute party politician.

The other countries of the Commonwealth have problems as difficult as those of the United Kingdom and a much smaller reservoir of talent upon which to call. It is therefore important to provide means by which able persons, unable or unwilling to take part in political activity, can be associated with the process of government. This is particularly true where the public service holds such an attraction as it does in Ceylon. Those who retire from the public service form a reservoir of excellent human material.

There is one special aspect of this problem. Even in Britain, the Prime Minister sometimes finds it necessary to have appointed to his Ministry a few persons who are not members of either House. There are two ways of doing it, both dependent on the existence of the House of Lords. The one is to raise the person concerned to the peerage. In this case, however, it is necessary to find an able deputy who can represent him in the House of Commons. The other method is to find a Member of Parliament, holding a safe seat, who is willing to accept a peerage. The party machinery can then ensure the election of the new Minister to the House of Commons.

This second method cannot always be used outside the United Kingdom, particularly in a plural society, because a seat which is safe for *X* is rarely equally safe for *Y*, even when he belongs to the same party. Persons are not often elected merely because they carry the party labels. They must be of the right race, religion, caste, etc., and very often some degree of personal influence is required. Accordingly, the Second Chamber may be the only means of bringing into the Government a person who will add weight or ability to its counsels. In India, Mr Nehru has strengthened his Government by bringing in a Minister of Finance through the Second Chamber, the Council of States. In a plural society, moreover, it may be necessary to secure a communal balance in the Cabinet. This happened in

Ceylon recently. It has become almost a convention that there shall be two Tamils and a Muslim in the Cabinet. For various reasons the present Prime Minister wanted to bring in a Tamil from outside Parliament. He therefore decided to appoint as Minister a Tamil Permanent Secretary, who resigned his post in the public service and was appointed to the Senate. This kind of problem is likely to arise quite often because the number of Tamils and Muslims in Parliament is always small; some will probably be members of the Opposition; and others may not be suitable for appointment as Ministers.

These examples from India and Ceylon raise another point. In the United Kingdom a Minister who is a peer cannot sit and speak in the House of Commons. On the other hand the Indian Constitution allows a Minister to speak in either House. A proposal to the same effect was made in Pakistan. In the draft Constitution proposed for Ceylon in 1943 there was to be a Senate and Ministers were to be allowed to speak in both Houses. For other reasons the scheme for a Senate was dropped, but a new scheme was substituted by the Soulbury Commission. Under that scheme, a Minister in the Senate cannot speak in the House of Representatives, and vice versa. It is generally held in Ceylon that this restriction was unfortunate and proposals for amending the Constitution are now under consideration.

These departures from the British precedent show that it is not applicable. One of the principal reasons for precedents of this kind is history; and history, it has been said, is an explanation but not a reason. In any case the other countries of the Commonwealth share that history only indirectly. It is also said in Britain that attendance at the other House would take much time and would add to the labour of Ministers who are already overburdened. Generally speaking, this does not apply outside Britain, where sessions are shorter and Ministerial duties less heavy. The attendance of Ministers places less responsibility upon Parliamentary Secretaries; and this is a defect because Parliamentary Secretaries ought to be able to gain experience. On the other hand this applies only to a few Parliamentary Secretaries, because most Ministers are in the House of Commons. The most important reason for not following the British precedent, however, is that the manpower available to a Prime Minister is usually limited and that he has to bring in Ministers through the Second Chamber because he cannot find enough suitable Ministers in the First Chamber.

Once it has been agreed that there ought to be a Second Chamber, it becomes possible to consider the system of representation as a whole. This is the kind of problem which requires detailed local knowledge. It should not be assumed that the system adopted in the United Kingdom is necessarily the best. As I have pointed out in previous talks, the people of the United Kingdom have become a very homogeneous people through centuries of constitutional development, but especially through the development of easy means of communication in the last hundred years, the raising of the standard of living, and the spread of education. The system of the single-member territorial constituency, or in other words the system of 'one vote, one value', is suited to its conditions. In a colony verging upon self-government these conditions do not obtain.

I have already discussed the advantages and disadvantages of communal representation. As a matter of general principle, one would say that it should be avoided if it can be avoided; and sometimes it can be avoided by a system of weighted representation, by giving a vote in one area greater weight than a vote in another area, and therefore in effect by giving the vote to a member of one community greater weight than the vote of another community. If one suggested that a European vote should count, say, one hundred times an African vote, one would no doubt be accused of colour prejudice, but that would not be the real reason. Generally speaking, in tropical countries the Europeans are few but their economic importance very considerable. Africans are numerous and their needs insistent; but their needs cannot be met unless European enterprise is sufficiently flourishing to provide the revenues from which the social services required by the Africans can be met. I do not assert that the way to solve the problem is to weight a European vote one hundred times: I merely say that if the problem is to enable Europeans and Africans to work together in partnership one should not exclude that kind of solution on theoretical grounds.

Nor is the problem necessarily one relating to a small but wealthy European class and a large but indigent African class. In some tropical countries there is a small but wealthy urban population and a large but impecunious rural population. In order to secure an efficient partnership between the trade and commerce of the towns on the one hand and the subsistence agriculture of the rural areas, on the other, it may be necessary to weight the urban vote. On the other hand, exactly the reverse may be needed, as it is in Ceylon. There the dense population of the west coast, which possesses both comparative wealth and the widest educational facilities, would dominate elections if one vote had one value. By increasing the value of a vote in the rural areas a balance has been struck, so that attention has to be paid not only to the interests of the people of the coast, but also to the interests of the people of the interior.

The decision to have a Second Chamber makes possible a double system of representation. In this respect there are complicating factors. One such factor, which I have already mentioned, is that a federal Constitution may be needed to give adequate emphasis to local needs and aspirations. Nobody would have a federal Constitution if it could be avoided, because it makes government complicated and gives wider powers of obstruction to the judiciary. Nevertheless, Canada, Australia, India and Pakistan have federal Constitutions, and it would no doubt be necessary to provide such Constitutions in East Africa, Central Africa and the West Indies. Where the federal system operates it is usually necessary to have the First Chamber representing the people of the Federation and the Second Chamber representing the States or Provinces. A similar arrangement may be needed even in a unitary Constitution if the Provinces are sufficiently powerful and distinct. This is the arrangement in South Africa, and it was proposed in Ceylon in 1943, though eventually a different arrangement was incorporated in the Constitution of 1946.

It is possible, however, to regard the Second Chamber as the representative body for the several communities, while the First Chamber represents the people as a whole. Such a suggestion was made in Ceylon in 1943. In Pakistan an attempt was made to balance the strength of East Pakistan and West Pakistan. It was proposed to have 'Rep. by Pop.' in the House of the People, East Pakistan having 165 seats and West Pakistan having 135 seats. In the Senate, or Second Chamber, however, East Pakistan was to have ten seats and West Pakistan forty seats. When the two Houses disagreed, and in certain other cases, there was to be a joint sitting. In such a joint sitting East Pakistan and

West Pakistan would each have 175 seats. It was, however, provided that a resolution would not pass unless it was supported by 30 per cent of the votes from each side. Consequently, neither East Pakistan nor West Pakistan could carry a proposal unless there was a strong minority favouring it in the other zone. As I have already explained, this complicated proposal was withdrawn and a single-chamber legislature established.

Another possibility is to add representation by nomination to representation by election. Many people regard this system as undemocratic and suggest that it savours of colonialism. If, however, an important section of opinion is too small to enable it to secure representation by election, nomination may be the only solution. In Ceylon it was feared that the Europeans and the Burghers, and perhaps the Muslims and the Indians, would not secure adequate representation by election. It was therefore agreed that the Governor-General, who since 1948 has been advised by the Prime Minister, should have power to nominate six persons to the House of Representatives, which contains ninety-five elected members. His powers are in fact wider, for half the members of the Senate are also nominated, and care has been taken to effect a reasonable communal distribution. Nor is it absolutely necessary that the Governor-General should act on the advice of the Prime Minister. It was at one time suggested that certain powers should be given to the President of Pakistan to be exercised by him in his discretion.

It will be seen that the variations on these lines are almost infinite. Almost invariably there are competing claims. It is not impossible to reach a compromise if it is realised that all these variations are consistent with democratic principles. The British Constitution is rightly admired by the peoples of the colonies, and a citizen of the United Kingdom must acknowledge the compliment to the wisdom of his forbears and contemporaries when others are so anxious to copy it. It must however be remembered that it has been adapted over centuries to meet the peculiar conditions of the United Kingdom, and that its principles are not of universal validity. A system of government is not necessarily undemocratic because it does not follow British precedents. On the contrary, the copying of those precedents in conditions different from those of the United Kingdom may result in the tyranny of the majority. The essential characteristic of the United Kingdom is that there is no permanent majority. If the people of England always continued to out-vote the peoples of Wales, Scotland and Northern Ireland, the British Constitution simply would not work. What makes it work is that the peoples of all four countries divide along the same party lines. One of the defects of colonial policy—if I may venture an opinion—before 1939 was that the Colonial Office and its local representatives expected colonial peoples, who had had no opportunity for acquiring experience in self-government, to develop the sort of political maturity which only experience can give. It is equally true that most nationalist politicians underestimate the difficulties. India will be the standing example for all time.

One other problem relating to the legislature remains to be discussed. What ought to be the qualification of members? Ought one to require, for instance, that they should be able to read and write English? Is it enough that they should be able to read and write some language? This kind of problem is never discussed in Britain because nearly everybody reads and writes English.

Let us think first of all in terms of spoken languages. It is little use making a speech unless other members can understand it. Moreover, the speech has to be taken down by stenographers and reproduced in the equivalent of Hansard. The development of a system of shorthand is, however, a difficult matter. In Ceylon experiments with Sinhalese shorthand are still being conducted, and no Member of Parliament has yet spoken in Tamil. Most speeches are in English, but eight per cent of the people read and write English, and every Member of Parliament can speak it although he is not required to do so. It is possible to operate systems of simultaneous translation, as in international conferences, but a legislature becomes a different sort of body when everybody is listening through headphones. No difficulty arises in Canada, where nearly every legislator understands both English and French, or in South Africa, where English and Afrikaans can both be used.

Next, we come to ability to read agenda papers, Bills, official reports. It is possible, as in Canada and South Africa, to use two languages, but even that is not easy. An English-speaking Member moves that certain words be added after the word 'not' in line 21 on page 15. An official of the House has then to draft an amendment into the second language which has the same effect. This is by no means easy, for no language is exactly translatable into another. In South Africa, where English and Afrikaans have equal validity, the official text is that signed by the Governor-General; and, in order to maintain parity, the Governor-General signs alternately the English text and the Afrikaans text. Sometimes the courts have to interpret the Afrikaans text when all the discussion took place on the English text, and there may be quite substantial differences between them.

In any case, it is plain that the Members of Parliament must be able to read the language, or one of the languages, in which the documents are drawn up. On the other hand, it may not be necessary so to prescribe. Pakistan proposed to require ability to read and write some language (not necessarily English), but neither India nor Ceylon has such a requirement. The reason is, I suppose, that an illiterate person is unlikely to be elected, unless he is a person of outstanding personality, in which case there is something to be said for having him in the legislature even if he cannot read the documents. What is more, literacy is a matter of degree. The common test is ability to read and write a short letter, but that sort of literacy is not enough for the understanding of a complicated Bill relating to such a subject as bills of exchange.

In these as in many other matters, flexibility is safest. If one cannot trust the electorate to operate a Constitution successfully the solution is to insert safeguards or other limitations on self-government. A mere handful of illiterates in a legislature of a hundred persons is not likely to obstruct government. The greater danger is that there will be too many slick orators who can read and write fluently but who also lack the maturity of judgment needed for self-government.

VIII

ADMINISTRATION

IF I were to follow a logical order, I should now discuss the Cabinet and the Executive Government generally. The logical order is not, however, the convenient order. The most difficult obstacle on the road to self-government is the staffing of the public services; and this needs emphasis because its importance is rarely appreciated. The difficulties in Burma and Indonesia are no doubt due in large measure to the consequences of Japanese occupation; there are similar difficulties in Malaya. Nevertheless, it seems also to be true that both countries lacked a cadre of experienced administrators capable of handling public affairs. Even Pakistan had difficulties, though it was able to draw upon the numerous Muslims in the public services of undivided India.

The notion that a country is governed by politicians is fallacious. The task of the politician is not to govern but to supervise government, to take decisions on questions of principle which are submitted to him, and to maintain a close relation between public opinion and the process of administration. The actual business of government is the function of professional administrators and technical experts. This elementary fact is masked in the United Kingdom by the stability of our Governments, the speed with which a new Government is formed when its predecessors resign, and the close relations which subsist between the officials and their political superiors. The French Republic shows the situation more clearly. The changes of Government are so frequent that few Englishmen have time to learn the name of the Prime Minister. There are, too, numerous periods of 'crisis', when superficially France has no Government at all. Nevertheless, the process of raising taxes and administering services is carried on without intermission and with very little change of policy.

This is equally true of Britain, though the machine functions so smoothly that it is hardly noticed. The part played in it by the politicians is important but small. The best example is the Post Office, a complicated organisation which can go on carrying the mails, running the telegraph and telephone systems, operating a Savings Bank, issuing licences, making social service payments, and performing a mass of miscellaneous functions, whether or not there is a Postmaster-General. It does over £3,000 million of business a year under the control of a permanent official, the Director-General, who has a vast organisation under him. Only a few questions of principle are submitted to the Postmaster-General. Indeed, it was said of one Postmaster-General that in the course of two years he took one decision only. I am sure that the story was a fiction and that it was designed to discredit his capacity as a Minister: nevertheless, this defamatory statement does illustrate the contrast between the running of a Government Department and the taking of the political decisions relating to that Department. The Minister is concerned with policy. He is responsible for the efficiency of his Ministry, but he does not administer. Under his political control there is a permanent official, usually called the Permanent Secretary, who runs the machine. That machine will consist of hundreds, or thousands, or even hundreds of thousands, of permanent officials. In Britain we call them 'civil servants', but in parts of the Commonwealth the term 'civil service' is restricted to the small group of senior administrative officers equivalent to the 'administrative class' in the Home Civil Service.

The pattern of the public service varies from country to country and even from colony to colony. Let me take the example of Ceylon as it was at the end of its colonial days, partly because it is a small country, but also because in respect of its public service it was almost a model colony. I must simplify the arrangements in order to make them intelligible.

At the lowest level were the labourers engaged on public works, irrigation schemes, the railways, etc. No standard of education was required, but many could read and write because the proportion of literates among males was about 60 per cent.

Above them were the peons or attendants who had had some education, usually in a vernacular language, and probably for as much as eight or nine years. Some of them could speak a little English, and a few could even read it. Ceylon was, however, again rather an exception, because about 10 per cent of the males could read and write English, and so a knowledge of spoken English was fairly widespread. It will be noticed that this class corresponds to the products of the elementary schools in England.

The next group were the clerks, who could read and write English and carry out routine administration under supervision. Most of them could type. Nearly all had passed the School Certificate Examination using English as medium. The best of this group became very good administrators. Every senior administrator relied heavily on his Chief Clerk. Indeed, it was sometimes said, with conscious exaggeration, that the Government of Ceylon was operated by the Chief Clerks. What is more, it was possible to promote persons from this group into the next group, the administrative grades. A few obtained positions of great responsibility.

With the clerical class must be associated persons in the technical grades, such as overseers engaged on public works, technical assistants in laboratories, technical staff on the railways, and so on. In addition to their general educational qualifications, they had had some technical training, perhaps on the job, perhaps under training schemes operated by Government Departments, perhaps in a technical college. The greatest weakness of the Ceylon system was, and still is, in this grade. The facilities for technical education were too few and the standard of technical skill was too low. Most Ceylonese feel, not unreasonably, that the economic progress of their country would have been greater and the standard of living higher if the Colonial Government had paid more attention to technical training.

Finally we come to what were called 'staff officers'. Anybody who picks up *Whitaker's Almanack* and studies the long lists published under 'Government and Public Officers' will see the varieties of job required. There were, however, two main groups. First, there were the general administrative officers called in Ceylon the 'Civil Service' and in Britain the 'Administrative Class'. Almost all of them were university graduates admitted to the service by an examination of university standard. There were, however, administrators outside the Civil Service of a somewhat lower academic level. Some were graduates and some had the equivalent of a London Intermediate qualification. The other large group consisted of professional men, such as doctors, lawyers, engineers, accountants, veterinary surgeons, scientists, and so on. Generally speaking they were required to have a qualification which would be recognised in England.

For the sake of simplicity I have left out some groups,

such as skilled workers, stenographers, policemen and police officers, customs appraisers, and so on. What I have tried to show is the relation between the public service and educational development. It will be noted, too, that the question whether the employees concerned are local people or imported people has not yet been discussed. This brings us to the root of the problem. In Ceylon it was called 'Ceylonisation'; in India it was called 'Indianisation'; and in Africa it is called 'Africanisation'—but in Africa the position is complicated by the existence of what are now called 'Asians' though they used to be called 'Asiatics'. I propose to use the term 'native' to mean a person born and bred in the country concerned. It has become perverted in South Africa and elsewhere to mean an African. I do not so use it. In my sense an Afrikaner or an English South African is a native, just as an Englishman is a native of England. I have to use it, in spite of possible misunderstanding, because I cannot keep talking about 'indigenous inhabitants'. In my sense a European or an Indian, born and bred in Kenya, is a native of Kenya.

It is obvious that every Colonial Government has to rely heavily on natives. Expatriates from the United Kingdom or elsewhere have to be paid high salaries in order to attract good men. They have to be given frequent home leave, and so a larger cadre has to be provided and passages have to be paid for. In tropical countries there is a rapid lowering of the standard of efficiency after the age of 50, and so the expense of pensions must be high. Imported officers expect a standard of comfort at least equal to that available in Britain. Expensive housing facilities have therefore to be provided. Also, there is usually no hire-purchase system in a colony, so that the Government has to provide loans for furniture and motor transport.

At the lower levels, therefore, the employment of natives is essential, and the problem in this respect—which I shall discuss later—is to develop an adequate educational system. At the higher levels, too, there is economic incentive towards the replacement of imported staff by native staff. There are, however, certain psychological factors which retard this development.

In spite of his world-wide responsibilities, the Englishman is very insular. He likes to mix with people of his own kind. He can live next door to a man for twenty years and never get beyond a polite 'good morning'. The Scots and the Irish are a little more flexible, but they have many English habits. There was once an Englishman who told me once a week that the colour bar began at Calais. I longed to tell him, though in fact I never had the courage, that the colour bar began at Temple Bar, for he knew a good deal more about countries east of Suez than he did about areas east of Temple Bar. It was not a colour bar at all: it was simply that he liked his own social circle and disliked all others. I am not sure that he approved of me, though he was willing to tolerate me because I was a Cambridge man.

The ordinary colonial civil servant is not such a Colonel Blimp. My experience came from Asia in the last stages of colonial rule: but I met very few officials who either practised or preached colour prejudice. It was simply that when they were off-duty they liked to go along to the European club and mix with people who shared their likes and dislikes, and who actually and metaphorically spoke their own language. If, however, there was a racially mixed staff, social contacts, particularly in a small out station, simply could not be avoided. The wives had to call, even if they found nothing to talk about. There had to be a few more or less formal dinner parties. The local Government

Officers' Club had to be racially mixed and therefore a little more formal than it had been when all the members were exiles, and therefore more British than the British. A few native officials, mostly graduates from Oxford and Cambridge, could become 'brown sahibs' and behave like Englishmen: but there was no reason why they should. A difference of social conventions compels a more formal atmosphere. In particular, except among the educated Chinese, the status of women is very different from what it is among Europeans. The sort of badinage which goes on among Europeans would neither be tolerated nor understood by most Asian and African women.

Consequently, though the necessity for employing natives even in the higher ranks has for long been accepted in theory, there has been some resistance to it in practice. Everybody agrees that local people should be appointed, but in some other station or some other Department. In this station or in this Department there are a dozen reasons why a European should be appointed. Some of these reasons are quite sound. For instance, for reasons which I should explain in my next talk, the European is often better suited for the job than a native with equivalent qualifications. This cannot be laid down as an absolute rule, because sometimes the reverse is true. The African or the Asian may have a much better knowledge of the people than the imported official. Again this is not an absolute rule, as those who have read Kipling's story of the Bengali who was appointed to the Frontier will know well.

Of course this resistance to Africanisation, or whatever it is, has to be overcome. Apart from other considerations, the economic development of the country requires that the heavy burden of official salaries be lightened. We are more concerned with the political considerations, and above all with the necessity for having a strong locally staffed public service before self-government is granted. This needs some explanation.

It cannot be said that the imported official is unwilling to serve under a local politician. There are plenty of examples in the Commonwealth. Nevertheless, some adjustments have to be made on both sides. The organisation of the colonial service is hierarchical. The official is responsible through the Head of his Department and the Colonial Secretary to the Governor and the Secretary of State. If he is senior enough, he may have to sit in the Legislative Council and work with local politicians, but at this stage the chain of responsibility is unchanged. In the simplest form of change-over to responsible government, the official becomes responsible through the Head of his Department and the Permanent Secretary to the Minister. Indeed, the reforms consequent upon responsible government may cause the disappearance of the Head of the Department as such. In the British system the Minister is the Head of the Department. Now, whether the Minister is European, Asian or African, the process of government under Ministerial control is very different from that under official control. The senior official is mainly concerned to do a good job. Naturally he wants to impress the Colonial Office, because his promotion depends upon it: but he knows that he will not go far with window-dressing because somebody will go behind the counter and somebody else will look at the books. Every politician is an expert at window-dressing because he has to maintain his prestige with the electors. He wants them to vote for him or the Government to which he belongs next time. Hence the official has to do window-dressing on behalf of his Minister even if he does not want to do any on his own behalf, and sometimes he does.

A story about window-dressing was told me by the first Prime Minister of Ceylon, Mr D. S. Senanayake. He once inspected a school, and the headmaster showed him with pride the magnificent school garden in which, by a happy coincidence, the vegetables and flowers were just reaching maturity. Mr Senanayake, who was himself a farmer, looked and listened but said nothing until he was leaving. He then took the headmaster aside and said to him: 'You know, those plants would do very much better if they had roots'.

I can, however, also tell you a story against Mr Senanayake. I accompanied the Prime Minister when he inspected a Government farm, and we saw some excellent fodder grass being grown for experimental purposes. As he went on to look at the cattle I dropped back and talked to the supervisor, who said to me: 'The old man insists on these experiments but they are all nonsense. We have to spend so much on fertilisers that it would be cheaper to import the grass. They are a waste of time because we can never grow this stuff economically'.

Mr Senanayake was far less inclined towards window-dressing than many of his officials. For instance, he was a rare bird in that he rarely took a press photographer with him. I once knew a Minister whose speciality was opening cottage hospitals. Since there was not enough furniture for them all, the Medical Department used to send on the furniture by lorry, furnish the hospital and make the beds, and make everything spick-and-span for the ceremony. When the Minister had made his speech and gone off, the beds were unmade, everything was packed up, and sent on to the next cottage hospital to be opened by the Minister. It sounds an incredible story but it is true in every particular.

There are less spectacular ways in which the official

has to be adaptable. There is, for instance, the ministerial conference at which technical matters have to be explained in order that the Minister may take a decision. The first Lord Kitchener was a famous example of the expert who found it difficult to explain himself to his political colleagues. There are, however, many less famous examples. Another technique which has to be employed is that of the memorandum. It is seldom realised that, whereas a lengthy document may be needed to convince a senior official, it must usually be short, plain and simple for a Minister because he has no time and less inclination to read a long rigmarole. What is more, a senior official must be able to draft documents which the Minister can sign. The Minister is a layman who is unwise to claim technical knowledge. He is also a politician who has a political reputation to maintain. Hence one must not only be able to say what the Minister wants said, but also say it in the manner in which the Minister wants to say it.

All this has no direct connection with the problem of superseding imported officials by local officials, but it has an indirect connection. If there is a rapid transition between colonial government and self-government it is necessary to replace one set of officials by another. Some will be transferred to other colonies, and some will be allowed to retire on favourable terms. Since in the long run native officials must be employed, it is wise to replace the imported officials by native officials wherever this is possible. It will not be possible in all cases. Ceylon imported quite a number of European officials after independence, though usually on short-term contracts.

There are, however, other reasons for effecting the change as soon as possible. Public opinion always demands it. Self-government looks spurious when local politicians have to work through imported officials. What is more, there is usually a strong communist group which is unwilling to admit that Lenin was wrong in his assertion that a colonial power could be forced to give up control but would not give it up voluntarily. Nor does an easy transition from colonial government to self-government suit communist tactics. It will therefore be said that the independence is a fake, that the British are continuing to govern through their stooges the democratic politicians, and that the white capitalists are simply paying the brown capitalists to look after their economic interests. Self-government has not only to be real; it has also to look real; and it does not look real if the same imported officials do the same jobs as before.

Moreover, the local politicians will probably have some suspicion of the European officials. The achievement of self-government almost invariably lags behind the demand for it. I shall discuss this point in a later talk; but it is almost inevitable that the process of change should be slower than the vocal nationalists require. Hence the nationalist politicians who achieve power will probably have spent years in criticising, and perhaps criticising fiercely, the very officials to whom they have to give instructions when they come into power. Naturally there is embarrassment on both sides.

It follows that the substitution of native officials for imported officials is an essential part of the process of developing self-government. Inevitably this takes a considerable time. A young man of 25, recently graduated, can rarely replace an administrator who has had thirty years' experience. Nobody likes to be selected for the young surgeon's first operation or to have his case pleaded by a young barrister who has just been called to the Bar. The process of administration is just as complicated, and there is great danger in putting it into inexperienced hands.

Unfortunately that will happen if self-government is accorded too quickly. It appears to have happened in Burma. Most of the officials in pre-war Burma were Europeans and Indians. When independence was achieved it was thought necessary to replace them by Burmans, few of whom had very much experience. In India the services had been in large measure Indianised by 1947, but a great many senior officials had to be pensioned off and professional experts were kept on for a short time only. It is generally agreed that, on the technical side, at least, there was some deterioration of standards. Pakistan recruited a number of the European officials who had served in undivided India, though not many are left eight years later. Ceylon effected the transfer most easily. The younger Europeans asked to be transferred to other colonies. Some of the older men retired on favourable terms—they were given credit for five years' service, so that an official who would normally have retired at fifty-five could retire at fifty on full pension. A small but important minority remained. Among the fourteen Permanent Secretaries, for instance, four were European, including the Secretary to the Treasury, the senior official in the public service. It happened, however, that Ceylon had a very large cadre of local officials. Very few non-Ceylonese had been recruited after 1934, and nearly all of them were professional men with special qualifications which were rare in Ceylon. In the medical service, for instance, every official was a Ceylonese because there had been good facilities for local training since 1870 and the Ceylonese had shown themselves to be good physicians, surgeons and obstetricians. The main weakness was in respect of engineers, a weakness due to inadequate facilities for local training and to the weakness of the general system of education in Ceylon, which gave excessive emphasis to examination qualifications and discouraged the acquisition of practical ability.

It will be seen that the problem is primarily educational, and accordingly I shall discuss it in my next talk. For the present it is necessary to emphasise that it is essential to have a public service which is staffed in large measure by local officials. To do this requires not only ample educational facilities, but also a whole generation of experience. To confer self-government merely because there are competent politicians available is to invite difficulties in practical administration.

IX

EDUCATIONAL DEVELOPMENT

OUR present approach to the educational problem is a very selective one. The development of self-government is not one of the objectives of education, but one of its inevitable consequences. We cannot educate the people of a colony without expecting them to ask for self-government. Conversely, we cannot confer self-government unless we develop educational institutions. The truth of neither proposition was fully realised in the nineteenth century. Generally speaking, the development of education was left to missionaries and to local initiative, though small grants were often paid from public funds. One result was that the wealthy section of the population, which was small but influential, obtained quite a good academic education through the medium of English. Little attention was paid to the mass of the population because the missionaries had no funds for education on the grand scale: and the quality of the education given through the local languages was generally poor because insufficient funds were available. Very little indeed was done for technical education.

The result was not only an unbalanced educational development, but also a strong nationalist movement, led by the English-educated, before the educational system was sufficiently developed to enable self-government to be granted. Africa is advancing more rapidly than Asia did: but experience in Asia suggests that nationalism becomes prominent in the third generation of the English-educated. The first generation was very small and consisted mainly of Eurasians and feudal landlords. The second generation were mainly clerks and interpreters, though a few obtained eminence in law and medicine. The third generation was much larger and began to infiltrate into the higher ranks of the public service: but it also produced the nationalist movement. The fourth generation achieved self-government; but meanwhile there had been for a whole generation antagonism between the rulers and the educated minority, that antagonism leading in India to the civil disobedience movement which was virtually a sort of rebellion.

Obviously the solution to that problem was to telescope the development. That is now being done. The fundamental difficulty of educational development has always been its cost. An adequate educational system in Ceylon, for instance, would probably cost about Rs 250 million, or £20 million, a year. This amounts to one-quarter of the total Government revenue in a good year, when the prices of primary products are high. Ceylon is, however, a rich country compared with most of the tropical colonies, and it is plain that if educational development is to be more rapid than it was in Ceylon substantial assistance must be provided from the funds of the United Kingdom. This has been realised since the Report of the Royal Commission on the West Indies in 1939, and education is one of the main fields of expenditure under the Colonial Development and Welfare Acts, by which the British taxpayer has provided large sums to assist in the development of the colonies.

My task is to discuss educational development in relation to the development of self-government; and this means that I must emphasise the importance of providing officials for the public services. I must however repeat that this is not the object of education. It has been alleged in Asia that the colonial governments in fact had no objective other than the provision of clerks and overseers for the public service. The allegation was, I believe, a product of the antagonism between nationalist politicians and their rulers and finds no support in history. Fortunately education needed for the social and economic development of a colony will also meet the needs of the public services.

Discussion about education in dependent territories always leads to debate on the language problem. It is, however, a difficult problem only where nationalist sentiment is so strong that it insists on the repudiation of English as a medium of administration. None of the other languages in use in the dependent territories, except Chinese, has been sufficiently developed to admit of its use for higher education. Both Malaya and Hong Kong are facing the problem of Chinese education, and that problem has become more acute since China became dominated by communism, for few of the books published in China can be used in Malaya or Hong Kong, while neither is capable of producing an adequate Chinese literature for itself. Moreover, both colonies must also use English; while if Chinese is used in Malaya (and later on in Sarawak and Borneo) there will inevitably be demands for the use of Malay. To have two media of instruction at the highest level among comparatively small populations will lead to numerous difficulties, and especially to financial difficulties, for higher education is necessarily expensive.

In Africa north of the Union, English is the inevitable medium of instruction at university level. It is equally inevitable that most primary education must be given in an African language. Hence the outline of the educational scheme is clear enough. There must be a very large number of primary schools using African languages, a proportionate number of post-primary schools emphasising English and, in the higher classes, using English as medium. There must also be one or more universities using English as medium. Only a very small proportion of the children entering the primary schools will reach the Universities. This needs to be emphasised, because over-enthusiastic nationalists often speak as if every fit student ought to be provided with the means for university education. This is flatly impossible for two reasons. The first is that even a comparatively rich country like the United Kingdom cannot afford to provide enough grammar schools and universities to give university education to 40 or 50 per cent of the population. In a comparatively undeveloped country the proportion must be very small indeed. The second reason is that the academic education given in high schools and universities is the wrong sort of education for the occupations that most students will have to follow. It sounds highly democratic to offer every young man the chance to become Chief Justice or Permanent Secretary to the Treasury; but it is not for the good of the country to have thousands of briefless barristers and hundreds of thousands of pass graduates who cannot get the sort of administrative jobs which they hoped to obtain. Not only will they be a nuisance to everybody, but also their ability cannot be used to develop the economy of their country.

Another section must be siphoned off into agricultural and technical education. Here again it must be remembered that the educational system, like the economic system, must be a broadly based pyramid. Agriculture is the main industry, but it needs at the base millions of peasants and labourers. Trained agriculturalists will inevitably be few, and agricultural graduates very few. Similarly in industry, which will inevitably develop slowly, there will be thousands of unskilled labourers, a great many skilled workers, a small proportion of technically trained assistants, and a few engineers.

Thus, the number siphoned off into agricultural schools, technical schools and technical colleges must be comparatively few. It is probably true to say, however, that in the past the provision made for technical education has been inadequate. In defence of the colonial administration it must be said that the relationship between supply and demand is a difficult one. It has been the practice to wait for the demand; but in this case the supply helps to create demand. Industries cannot be developed until there are people anxious to develop them and, except among the Chinese, the anxiety does not prevail widely because ambitious young men do not know how to start. Besides, there is often a prejudice against manual labour, especially where the caste system prevails; and an overseer or even an engineer who cannot do a job with his own hands is not likely to be very effective. In the result, the territory tends to have a vast base of unskilled labour and an apex of engineers and agricultural experts, but few skilled workers and technicians in between.

Another need on which insufficient emphasis has been laid is for trained teachers. The primary schools need teachers trained through the medium of the local languages. Since in most languages the means for training in those languages, particularly books, is lacking, it follows that the teachers must be bilingual in English and the local language. This is difficult to obtain, because those who learn English in the high school do not want to go back to teach in the primary schools: they prefer to go on to the University and compete for much more highly paid jobs. It is true that the failures will be willing to teach; but they are not the best people for this purpose and in any case they will have neglected the local languages in order to excel in English. The provision of teachers for the high schools is easier. Some will be trained in training colleges; others will be graduates who have received special training in Education.

The problem has been discussed in relation to economic needs generally. It may now be pointed out that the needs of the public service have also been met. The primary schools meet the demand for employees at the lowest level. The high schools provide clerks, typists and stenographers. The technical schools provide skilled workers and mechanics. The agricultural colleges and technical colleges provide overseers, instructors and technicians. The university provides administrators, scientists and professional experts like doctors, dental surgeons, engineers, veterinary surgeons, agricultural scientists, etc.

A complete educational structure cannot be provided in a single generation. It is seldom realised, too, that education at each level depends upon the level above. The primary schools need teachers educated in the high schools; the high schools need teachers educated in the university. The technical schools require teachers trained in the technical colleges; the technical colleges require engineers and scientists from the university. On the other hand, it is also true that the higher level depends upon the level below. The high schools and the technical schools take pupils from the primary schools; the university and the technical colleges take pupils from the high schools. It is an old problem. There are no eggs without hens and no hens without eggs.

The development is inevitably slow, and it cannot be done without outside assistance. That assistance came in the first instance from the missionaries, who started schools and trained their own teachers. More recently

Governments have stepped in and have imported teachers, especially for the training colleges. As soon as a reasonably good high school, or collection of high schools, is available, it is possible to send students abroad. What is more, wealthier parents are able to send their sons at their own expense. Almost without exception the senior public servants in Ceylon are Ceylonese educated in English universities. This is, however, a slow and expensive process. It is clear that a university, or at least a university college, ought to be established as soon as possible.

It may be noted that this step can be taken too early. In 1857 three universities were established in India, those of Bombay, Calcutta and Madras. They were copied from the then University of London, which was by no means a good model. Indeed, the University of London has spent much of its effort since 1857 in reforming itself into the effective and powerful corporation now administered from Bloomsbury. In spite of the fact that the Indian system so adopted in 1857 has often been condemned, notably by the Sadler Commission in 1919 and the Radhakrishnan Commission in 1952, it has never been reformed because the vested interests are too numerous and too powerful and vast sums of money would be needed. Also, the three Indian universities were created before an adequate high school system had been established. Their admission standards had to be low and, in spite of their constant efforts to raise them, their standards are still low. The lesson to be learned from India, which the best Indian educationists would themselves emphasise, is that premature development of university education is unwise.

On the other hand, development in Ceylon was too slow. In one respect Ceylon was very successful. By 1941 every medical practitioner in the Government service was a Ceylonese, and it is worth while to ask why. The explanation is that the Ceylon Medical College, which is now incorporated in the University of Ceylon, was founded in 1870. Its original function was to train not qualified doctors but unqualified medical assistants. By drawing upon the hospital staff, European and Ceylonese, for its teaching, it was able to secure recognition from the General Medical Council in 1888, and thus to confer a registrable qualification upon its successful students. This relationship with a professional body in the United Kingdom was important because, as British standards were raised, Ceylon standards had to follow them. When the College was warned that its standards were falling behind, the Government was compelled to find the funds for new buildings, better equipment and more staff.

In other respects the development of university education was unnecessarily delayed, perhaps by as much as twenty years. In one respect, however, the Ceylon University College followed the example of the Ceylon Medical College. It tied its standards to those of England by preparing for London examinations. The syllabuses were not very satisfactory in Ceylon conditions, and the London examinations had a harmful effect on the schools. Even now the consequences of those defects have not been overcome. Nevertheless, when the University of Ceylon was created in 1942 it had no doubt about its standards. In Arts and Science it insisted upon those of the University of London: in Medicine it followed closely the recommendations of the General Medical Council. These standards are being maintained by the use of external examiners from the United Kingdom.

Fortunately the lesson of Ceylon was learned in London. In 1945 the Secretary of State for the Colonies appointed a Commission on Higher Education in the Colonies. A separate Commission was appointed for the West Indies, and two years later, when Malaya had been freed from Japanese occupation, another Commission was appointed for Malaya.

In Malaya, where the College of Medicine and Raffles College had been created before the war, it was possible to establish a University forthwith. Elsewhere it was necessary to begin with university colleges, and these have now been established in the West Indies, the Gold Coast, Nigeria, East Africa, the Sudan and Rhodesia. They teach for London examinations; but the defects evident in Ceylon have been overcome by creating a 'special relationship' under which local examiners, assisted by London examiners, set papers on local syllabuses. Further, an advisory body called the Inter-University Council for Higher Education Overseas, representing the universities of the United Kingdom and the Colonies, was created. Its advice is sought by, and is freely given to, not only the six university colleges mentioned above, but also the Universities of Malta, Hong Kong and Malaya.

The colonies could not, however, support these universities and university colleges without substantial financial assistance from the United Kingdom. This is now available through the Colonial Development and Welfare Acts and is provided on the advice of the Colonial Universities Grants Committee, which in turn consults the Inter-University Council for Higher Education Overseas.

It should be added that there has been a similar development, though by no means so spectacular, in relation to technical education. The result is that, while the colonies still recruit teachers and educational administrators from the United Kingdom, the United

Kingdom has been providing staff, money, advice and (through the University of London) educational standards for universities and university colleges which will provide the officials of the next generation. At the same time, a very large number of colonial students have been and are being educated in the universities of the United Kingdom and a smaller number in the universities of the United States, Canada and Australia. From East Africa many Indian students go to universities in India.

It follows that there should be no difficulty in the next generation in filling most official posts with local men. The process can be accelerated but not hurried. It can be accelerated by giving preference to local men where they are available and have equivalent qualifications. Ceylon did this in 1934 by requiring a resolution of the State Council whenever a post was to be filled from abroad otherwise than by normal promotion. This was not a good method because it led to canvassing, and occasionally to even less ethical methods, in the legislature. On the other hand, it was effective, so that when Ceylon obtained self-government in 1947, it was unnecessary to dismiss any staff at all. Some left of their own accord; but those European officers who had done good work and had proved themselves adaptable to the new conditions were actually pressed to stay. Since 1947 their number has diminished through normal retirements and resignations, and there are now only six European officers in the administrative branch of the service, while they are even fewer in the technical services.

Occasionally Ceylon has difficulty in finding a local candidate with good enough qualifications and experience. In many respects the experience obtainable in Ceylon is rather limited. The standard of education depends in part on the standards attained in the schools and the university, but it also depends on the quality of home education. This is in many cases rather low because educational developments have proceeded so rapidly that the present generation is much ahead of the previous generation, while the previous generation was much ahead of the one before. The quality of home education depends on the degree to which parents are educated, the availability of toys, books, periodicals and newspapers, the accessibility of public libraries, museums, art galleries and film shows. Each generation depends upon the standard of education of its predecessor. What is more, it depends upon the standard of living in the home, because means of education are expensive. It follows that educational development is a slow process and that it depends in large measure on economic development. No matter how much money and effort are spent on a primitive tribe, several generations have to pass before modern European standards can be attained. Even where the community is not primitive, but merely underprivileged, like the scheduled castes in India, only the exceptional boy or girl can expect to compete with boys from the families of learned Brahmins or the Europeanised families of Bombay. Home education is so inferior that school education cannot be fully effective: and school education depends not only on the standards of the teachers but also on the standards of the pupils. By conscious effort, the standard of each generation can be raised above that of its predecessor but one cannot press the experience of centuries into one generation or even into two generations.

Even where there are no such problems, however, there are difficulties in gaining experience. For instance, the best surgeons in Ceylon are as good as the best surgeons elsewhere. There are, however, few of them because a small country cannot maintain many skilled surgeons. They cannot see in Ceylon the wide range of operations available in London or New York. Special fields like thoracic or neurological surgery may be closed to them because they have not shared the experience gained by surgeons elsewhere. There are two ways of meeting this problem. One is to send Ceylonese surgeons abroad at frequent intervals so that they can acquire a broader experience. The other is to bring experts to Ceylon. Both methods have to be used.

We may perhaps put the problem in this way. There may be a dozen Fellows of the Royal College of Surgeons in Ceylon, but several thousand in England. There may be six pathologists in Ceylon but several hundred in England. The proportions in cognate fields are similar. These expert groups react on each other and produce the developments in surgery which give countries like the United Kingdom, the United States, Switzerland, Austria, etc., such pre-eminence. Moreover quality creates quality. Just as one cannot expect an athlete to break a world record unless he races against athletes of Olympic standard, so one cannot expect a surgeon to be world-famous unless he works in a stimulating environment. Hence with a country like Ceylon it is necessary continually to inject experience by movement both ways, of local experts to foreign countries, and of foreign experts into the territory.

This requirement of a highly qualified and experienced body of administrators and technical experts is perhaps the most difficult on the road to self-government. It is easy to produce politicians, though it is not always easy to find those who possess wisdom and judgment. The provision of a competent cadre of officials is a more difficult matter because it cannot be hurried and the speed depends less on the policy of the colonial power than on the cultural and economic standards of the country. In applying precedents from Asia it must be remembered that the mass of the peoples of India, Pakistan and Ceylon, though generally at a low cultural and economic level, does retain substantial relics of ancient and highly developed cultures. There are primitive tribes in Asia, but most of them are centuries beyond the Stone Age.

X

EXECUTIVE GOVERNMENT

THE business of government is not very different from any other business. It is on a vaster scale and the consequences of failure are much more serious. The vastness of the scale makes it essential that there should be a highly skilled public service; and, indeed, without it self-government is quite unthinkable. On the other hand, once the skilled public service has been provided it ought not to be difficult to secure Ministers who possess the qualities needed for taking decisions. That public service, too, should be strong enough to prevent Ministers from leading the way towards national disaster provided—and it is an important proviso—the Ministers are anxious to avoid national disaster.

It is not very easy to say what are the qualities required by a statesman. If we take examples from Britain alone we see how different are the politicians to whom history has given awards of merit. There was William Pitt, the son of the great Earl of Chatham, who went to Cambridge at the age of 13 and became Prime Minister at the age of 23, defying the majority until he could win a majority; there was Sir Robert Peel, the son of a manufacturer, a brilliant Oxford scholar, perhaps our ablest administrator, the politician who introduced the matter-of-fact style of speaking to the House of Commons, but a politician who twice split his party. There was William Ewart Gladstone, who had much the same background, but who had a sort of torrential eloquence which he poured out not only in Parliament but on the public platform, and who dominated his Cabinets as no man had done before or has done since. There was his opponent, Benjamin Disraeli, the son of a Jewish writer, a flamboyant actor on the public stage who was nevertheless an astute politician. There was A. J. Balfour, a Scottish philosopher from Cambridge, no orator at all, but a perfect chairman and draftsman of exquisite formulae. There was David Lloyd George, the little Welsh radical solicitor, a virulent controversialist who somehow—nobody quite knows how—managed to win a great war. And there is Sir Winston Churchill who has tried many things and has succeeded in them all, except in the passing of examinations, a politician who has twice changed his party, a politician whom nobody could trust and yet a politician who got a united nation behind him and defeated the greatest enemy that Britain ever had.

What had those in common? I suspect that they had nothing in common except ability out of the ordinary: but we have also had successful Prime Ministers of ordinary ability, like the first Earl Russell, Lord Aberdeen, Sir Henry Campbell-Bannerman, Stanley Baldwin and Lord Attlee. If I try to explain what seems to me to be the qualities which a statesman ought to possess, I shall certainly run into difficulties because to every rule there is an exception. Nevertheless, the attempt must be made. I shall give these qualities not in order of importance, but as they arise through the association of one idea with another.

The first quality is patriotism. Politicians are normally ambitious people, but if they are concerned only with power and prestige they will never succeed in getting the degree of support needed to operate Cabinet government. This is perhaps the easiest quality to find in a colony which is on the verge of self-government because it will not be on the verge of self-government unless it has a strong nationalist movement. Indeed, it may be so strong as to become ultra-nationalist, to develop ideas of isolationism and self-sufficiency which are quite unsuited to a modern State and particularly unsuited to a country which has been dependent upon a colonial power. 'Ourselves alone' is not a practicable policy.

This patriotism may have a dangerous partisan bias, especially in a plural society. Men cannot easily forget their ancestral loyalties, the race, religion, caste, tribe or clan to which they belong. Communalism is not inconsistent with patriotism because patriotism may be fundamentally communal. I have explained in a previous talk the importance of what I have called 'the larger patriotism'. It is essential that a Government should be able to attract the support of all sections of the community. A politician who plays upon communal prejudices in order to secure himself in power is, in the long term, a traitor to his country.

Patriotism implies, too, a sense of responsibility not merely to the party, or to the people as they are now, but to generations yet unborn. This is a rarer quality because it is very easy for a politician to think in terms of the next election. It is easy, too, for him to persuade himself that the interest of his country requires him to keep himself in power by taking a popular decision and ignoring its ultimate consequences. Some of the ablest politicians are excellent improvisers. They take no thought for the morrow not because tomorrow can take care of itself, but because they hope and indeed expect that tomorrow they can find a way out of any difficulty that they may have created. Such politicians are not statesmen, and eventually they fall. When they do, they may bring many of their fellow-countrymen with them.

This sense of responsibility may, however, go too far. If every Minister thought out fully the consequences of the decisions, he would never take a decision. He has a staff to guide him, and they ought to be able to put the alternatives in such a form that he can take a decision. Nevertheless, the choice may be and often is a choice between bad alternatives. Nor can any Minister be given all the information that he would like to have. He does not know and cannot be told whether there will be a flood next week or a drought next year. He can only guess whether the price of wheat or cotton or rubber or maize will go up next year or down. He has to take decisions of the utmost importance on inadequate information; and he has to take them quickly, knowing that the consequences may be far-reaching.

This requires a moral courage which seems to be quite rare. There is a noticeable tendency in every public service to pass on the responsibility; but when it comes to the top it can go no further. The Minister or the Cabinet must decide. The nervous strain on a sensitive and patriotic person may be considerable, particularly if the risks are great and the decisions unpalatable. A Prime Minister once told me that he had to take decisions every day, knowing that nine-tenths of them might be wrong. Perhaps he exaggerated because, as I pointed out to him, he had a fifty-fifty chance of being right. Actually the chances are higher. He has behind him an efficient public service, and he would not hold office if he had not rare qualities of judgment. Those qualities are very difficult to define. They seem to depend not merely on experience and accumulated wisdom, but also on intuition. One always doubts whether Lloyd George had, or Sir Winston Churchill has, the sort of judgment manifested by A. J. Balfour or Stanley Baldwin or even, probably, Lord Attlee. Their special quality seems to be intuition. I often saw this quality working in the first Prime Minister of Ceylon, Mr D. S. Senanayake. He had no academic background worth mentioning; his experience was limited to running an estate, managing tough plumbago miners, making very poor speeches in antagonism to British rule, and finally acting as Minister of Agriculture for a number of years. He read very little and he had a vast range of miscellaneous functions to perform. Nevertheless he could take a decision, even in a complicated matter of law or economics, on the spur of the moment. He would tell his advisers in a few halting words—for he was almost inarticulate—what it was he wanted. When the draft came back to him he would have it read over to him and would listen in silence until a point arose with which he disagreed. He did not need to pause and weigh the advantages and disadvantages. He would simply say 'I mean to say' or ''s matter of fact' – phrases which meant that he disliked that line of argument or that conclusion and that it must be changed.

This kind of intuition is rare; but where it exists it is founded upon wisdom and experience. Very little experience can be obtained by political debates and none at all by fiery speeches to popular audiences. A mature parliamentary machine like that of the United Kingdom does enable wisdom to be exhibited, because every Member knows whether another Member is talking sense or merely ranting. On the other hand it does not create wisdom; and indeed nobody knows how it is created. It just grows, like Topsy. It is possible to claim that the British taught wisdom to Mr Jawaharlal Nehru by putting him in gaol: but very often those who exhibit the highest wisdom never have time to think things out. Nor do those who have thought things out necessarily possess wisdom. In the field of nationalist politics the best example was perhaps Mahatma Gandhi, who may have been a saint but was certainly not a wise one.

On the other hand, the good statesman must have one quality which Mahatma Gandhi certainly possessed, the capacity to make people believe in him and follow him. Normally this requires not saintliness but transparent honesty. Yet this is not enough, for Neville Chamberlain was transparently honest, though he never secured the enthusiastic support even of his own party, while Disraeli, who gave the impression of being a clever *poseur* and had few of the characteristics of a good conservative, is almost the patron saint of the Conservative Party.

It is difficult to draw lessons from this history. Parliamentary institutions work well where they have worked well. A tradition develops to which each generation conforms. In handing responsibility to a new parliamentary system one must necessarily take risks. It is impossible to expect that colonial politicians will develop overnight the traditions which Britain has accumulated over centuries. The point at which risks can reasonably be taken must invariably be a matter of controversy. It is not unreasonable to allege that before 1945 progress was too slow and cautious. What is more, that slowness and caution led impatient politicians to attribute different motives, to allege that Britain was giving slowly because British administrators were anxious to keep power in their own hands. I doubt whether this was so, and I feel certain that it was not so in Ceylon. There the accident of history made me a spectator with a ring-side seat. I knew the local officials and even had some acquaintance with those in the Colonial Office. I also knew the local politicians and sympathised with their aspirations. The officials saw difficulties which did in fact occur, and which had to be overcome. No doubt they exaggerated them but they did so honestly. On the other hand, the local politicians quite honestly suspected the motives of the colonial rulers, though I am sure that the suspicions were unjust.

In India both the difficulties and the suspicions were far greater. Nobody, whether in Britain or in India, can look back with pride on the period of Indian history between 1940 and 1945. It is easy to be wise after the event and to say that the problem could have been solved by agreement in India as it was in Ceylon. Indeed, it may be alleged that it was solved in Ceylon by a series of happy accidents. Even so, it is plain that the example to be followed is not that of India but that of Ceylon. There is no doubt of Britain's anxiety to develop self-governing institutions in the colonies. There is equally no doubt of the anxiety of colonial politicians to solve the problems which hinder their advance to self-government. Those problems can be solved by collaboration, but they may take time. They cannot be solved by a mere repudiation of 'colonialism'.

Perhaps we may leave this nebulous atmosphere of political controversy and consider the practical problems of Cabinet government. It is hardly necessary to argue whether it ought to be Cabinet government. Colonial politicians have seen it operating in the United Kingdom. Many of them have studied its working as described in the books. As students they may have answered examination questions about the relative merits of Presidential government and Cabinet government: but in a colony under British rule Presidential government is academic while Cabinet government is real. What is more, Cabinet government is a flexible system capable of adaptation to varying circumstances. Even Canada, under the shadow of the great American nation, has adopted a Constitution 'similar in principle to that of the United Kingdom'. Nor has it seen anything in the United States which encourages a change. Indeed, Canada exhibits the flexibility of the Cabinet system. A President of Canada would be either English-Canadian or French-Canadian. In the Canadian Cabinet some are English and some are French. Whether the Prime Minister is English or French depends not on the balance of votes but on the capacity as politicians of the persons concerned. The names of the Canadian Prime Ministers are significant—Sir John MacDonald, Sir Wilfrid Laurier, Sir Robert Borden, Mr Mackenzie King, Mr St Laurent—three English-Canadians and two French-Canadians. Cabinet government, being flexible, is particularly suited to a plural society.

In such a plural society Cabinets can be mixed in respect of race, religion, caste, tribe or clan. In Ceylon it is usual to have at least two Tamils and one Muslim. The Indian Cabinet is drawn from the several racial groups of India. Pakistan has to give due weight both to East Pakistan and to West Pakistan. Even so, the principle of collective responsibility is essential. There will be divisions of opinion within a Cabinet, but in the end there must be an acceptable decision which is put to the legislature with the full weight of a Cabinet decision and carried by the strength of the Cabinet's majority. If this is not done it is impossible to follow a consistent policy.

This implies some sort of party system. Fortunately this is not difficult to attain at the outset, for the various groups agitating for self-government tend to coalesce. In India the Congress, which included nearly all sections of democratic opinion, was able to form a Government not only in the Union, but also in the States. It is tending to shed its wings and to become a solid party which may be described in continental terms as 'right centre'. In Pakistan the Muslim League, which was responsible for the creation of the Dominion, remained in power for seven years, though it has recently lost control of East Pakistan and has no party majority in the Constituent Assembly. In Ceylon, where there were no parties before independence, the United National Party was formed in anticipation of independence and won the elections of 1947 and 1952.

In none of these three countries has a strong Opposition party appeared. In India the Congress might be defeated by a coalition, as it was in Travancore-Cochin and Andhra. The defeat of the Muslim League in East Pakistan was brought about by a coalition. In Ceylon the Opposition parties are mere splinter-groups. One reason is to be found in the strength of the communist parties. They are always willing, for tactical reasons, to join other parties in what is called a 'common front', but their purpose is disruptive. They have no anxiety to enable the Constitution to function. They merely want to get into a strong enough position to be able to overthrow it. The non-communist Opposition groups, on the other hand, are splinter-groups which have split off from the main party.

This is already a dangerous situation. If the ruling party—the Congress in India, the Muslim League in Pakistan, and the United National Party in Ceylon—loses its majority there is no alternative Government. This no doubt gives it electoral strength, for the solid elector has either to vote for it or to risk chaos. On the other hand, the continued dominance of one party tends to cause splits inside the governing party. In Britain, if the Conservative Party becomes divided, there is bound to be a Labour Government. If a serious split occurs in the Labour Party there is bound to be a Conservative Government. The system of one-party rule which operates in India, Pakistan and Ceylon encourages intrigue within the Cabinet. One must not draw too favourable conclusions from the success of Cabinet government in India, Pakistan and Ceylon, because the test of time has not yet been imposed and experience is too short.

One cannot, however, expect a colony to wait for self-government until it has developed a firm party system. Such a system is not the condition precedent to Cabinet government but a consequence which flows from it. Indeed, the struggle for self-government discourages the formation of competing parties. All groups tend to coalesce into a single nationalist party like the Indian National Congress, which contained all sections of opinion from extreme right to extreme left because all were agreed on Indian independence. On the other hand, the minority groups, while anxious for self-government, have their own claims to urge against the majority group. The majority party may thus become a communal group. This was the tragedy of undivided India. The Muslim League was as anxious for independence as the Congress; on the other hand it had its own claims against the Congress which the Congress would not accept.

With this kind of problem the Colonial Government cannot deal. Indeed it is an obstruction to agreement simply because, being in power, its support is sought by the communal groups. There is, however, one danger against which the Colonial Government has to protect the colony. *Ex hypothesi* the competing parties are inexperienced. I shall discuss in my next talk the methods by which experience can be acquired in the transition between colonial government and self-government. Experience has shown, however, that that transition cannot be long: hence inexperience must be assumed as an axiom.

Since all parties are combined against the Colonial Government, the communists have every argument for a common front. Lacking experience of communist methods, the nationalist groups will probably accept their assistance. In accordance with their usual technique, the communists will take the lead in the nationalist front. Nevertheless their purpose is disruptive. They intend to achieve not democratic self-government but the dictatorship of the communist party. Is there any reason why the Colonial Government should accept that situation? I think there is none. What Britain is pledged to give is democratic self-government, and as soon as that system can be establised. It is not pledged to the establishment of a communist dictatorship. It is entitled to say that British rule, whatever its defects, is designed for the benefit of the people of the colony. In spite of some serious mistakes, to which attention is always—quite reasonably—drawn by nationalist politicians, it has usually succeeded in its aim. It created, for instance, the nations of India, Pakistan and Ceylon, for those nations were communal fragments when Britain took over. Britain therefore has no justification for abdicating in favour of a communist dictatorship. If the people of the colony cannot govern themselves, the solution is to retain colonial government until they can.

XI

THE DILEMMA OF REPRESENTATIVE GOVERNMENT

THOSE who criticise British colonial government without studying it draw a sharp contrast between 'colonialism' on the one hand and 'self-government' or 'freedom' or 'independence' on the other. No such sharp contrast can be drawn. There are very few dependent territories in which the inhabitants play no part at all in their own government. There are tribal areas in which the tribes govern themselves under the benevolent dictatorship of a Governor or High Commissioner; but if this is 'colonialism' India and Pakistan are colonial powers, for they have areas governed in very much the same way. For instance, India has listed in its Constitution certain 'States' which are not federated States of the Indian Union, but which are governed more or less directly by the Government of India. Such a 'State' may have an elected legislature, a legislature which is partly elected by the people and partly nominated by the Government of India, or a legislature which is wholly nominated. It may have a Council of Ministers, or a Council of Advisers, or be administered autocratically from New Delhi. These constitutional provisions are, in fact, simply formulations of British colonial practice. Further, there are territories in India, some of them with a tribal organisation not fundamentally different from that which prevails in certain parts of Africa, which are governed by the Government of India much as the protectorates of Africa are governed by the Government of the United Kingdom. There is, however, one difference between 'British colonialism' and 'Indian colonialism', and it is due to geography. The dependent peoples of India are part of the Union; they are Indian citizens, and the objective is to give them the same rights and privileges as other Indian citizens. The citizens of British colonies are British subjects (though the citizens of protectorates are British-protected persons); but the objective is not to bring them within the United Kingdom but to convert their territories into independent countries. India's problem is therefore easier; for whereas in due course British officials must leave Uganda or Malaya, it will not be considered inappropriate for Indian officials from Madras or Bengal to continue in the Andaman Islands or the Naga Hills.

If the degree of influence brought to bear on the process of government by the inhabitants is a sign of progress, one must say that the territories of the Commonwealth are at every stage of progress from benevolent autocracy to complete independence. What is more, there is constant movement up the scale. One sign of this progress is that the works of reference are always out of date. The legal staff of the Colonial Office every year produces constitutions and constitutional amendments designed to enable the inhabitants to play a greater part in their government. Occasionally, unfortunately, there has to be a step backwards. Sometimes it is taken by the inhabitants themselves, as in some of the West Indian colonies in the middle of the nineteenth century. More often internal dissension or a threat of anarchy leads to intervention by the Government of the United Kingdom, as in Jamaica, Malta and British Guiana.

It must be remembered that most colonial territories are, socially, artificial units created by British rule, and that the prospect of the removal of that rule sometimes leads to disruption. Ceylon was a unified kingdom a thousand years ago, but when the Portuguese arrived in 1505 there were three kingdoms, and the island was not united under a single sovereignty until 1815. The people of Ceylon think of themselves as 'Ceylonese' because of British rule; but they also think of themselves as Sinhalese and Tamils, and the Sinhalese recognise a distinction between the Kandyan and the low-country Sinhalese. India, with or without Pakistan, never was a political unit until Britain made it so. A few emperors, like Asoka and some of the Mughals, exercised a wide jurisdiction for a short period, but they never held the whole sub-continent. India until British rule was a kaleidoscope of sovereignties, shaken up from time to time. Moreover British sovereignty was acquired piecemeal and the territory was never reorganized, so that both India and Pakistan have a medley of Provinces and States which will create political problems for generations. In Africa most of the units are even more artificial, since they are frequently mere congeries of tribes.

Fervent nationalists often forget that they are an educated minority whose nationalism derives from the English education which they have received under British rule, and that the mass of the people is more likely to abide by its traditional loyalties. Hence the removal of British rule does not at once produce a comprehensive national patriotism. On the contrary, it may lead to sectional agitation. It is one thing for the British to rule Hindu and Muslim alike; it is another for the Hindus to rule the Muslims. So, too, among the Muslims: it is one thing for the British to rule the Muslims and another for the Punjabi Muslims to rule the Sindhi Muslims. The acceptance of a nationalist thesis by a small middle class does not involve the disappearance of sectional loyalties; and if self-government is pushed on too fast these sectional loyalties may become fissiparous. Because this argument tends to the lengthening of British rule, it is often alleged that the British encourage these fissiparous loyalties. If the problem exists, however, it is not solved merely by 'blaming the British'. It is now plain that the Indian National Congress seriously underestimated the strength of Islamic sentiment and that its intransigeance on this issue actually helped in the establishment of Pakistan. Even in 1955 the British were being blamed for the suspicions of the Punjabis which were clearly exhibited by the other peoples of West Pakistan. Many other examples could be cited. The purpose of these observations is not to defend British rule or to complain of the practice of blaming them, but merely to point out that self-government can move too fast for the movement of opinion. There are, too, personal ambitions which sometimes cause administrative chaos and compel intervention. India and Pakistan should now have no difficulty in understanding the problem, for recently India suspended the Constitution of Andhra, while Pakistan has within the space of seven years suspended Provincial Constitutions four times.

To say that there is a consistent pattern in the development would be to oversimplify. Constitutional development is always empirical because the dependent territories have different origins and different traditions. Moreover, reliance is placed on the man on the spot, usually the Governor, who consults local opinion. In consequence, there is a constant process of experimentation. The experience of one territory is used in another: but it is not assumed that the two territories ought to develop similar institutions. Nevertheless, I cannot in a series of talks like this give an account of all the variations which have been adopted in the numerous territories under British control. Nor indeed am I competent to do so; for I believe that one cannot properly discuss the constitutional progress of a territory by studying its paper Constitutions. There is always a background of knowledge and experience which explains them. Jeremy Bentham must go not only to Mexico but also to British Honduras, Sierra Leone, Fiji and all the other places whose stamps we so much admired when we were younger. I have not been to any of them: but I would like to take you to the hypothetical colony of Arcadia, which has had an unusually regular constitutional history since it was captured from the French—or was it the Spaniards or the Dutch?—during the Napoleonic wars.

As soon as the Crown's possession was ratified by the treaty of peace, a Governor was sent out with a Commission to act as Governor and Commander-in-Chief. Arcadia had never known self-government, at least within living memory. Its inhabitants were mostly illiterate peasants with a tribal organisation and a system of native law which satisfied most of their simple needs. The Governor was not expected to disturb these arrangements, but he had to take steps to organise the revenue, build roads, and generally open up the colony. If a profitable trade could be developed, so much the better. Trade, it may be remembered, benefits both those who buy and those who sell. Later on, when a nationalist movement developed in Arcadia, it was alleged that when British traders bought or sold they were agents of imperialism but that when the local population bought and sold they were being exploited by hard-faced capitalists. A local wit then started a movement for the freedom of the United Kingdom from 'imperialist exploitation' on the ground that when the local traders sold to and bought from British people they were hard-faced capitalists grinding the faces of the poor people of Britain. He was heard in disapproving silence and shortly afterwards left the country.

The Governor was in a sense an autocrat, but he took care not to antagonise local opinion, in so far as there was any. He had a few European officials to help him and a couple of companies of troops in glaring red uniforms who mounted guard when they were not laid low with smallpox, cholera, malaria, dysentery, or the very potent local liquor. If anybody had started a revolution, however, the Governor would be the first to be buried in the cemetery thoughtfully provided by the padre he had brought out with him. Besides, if any trouble started, Whitehall would send him what in the official slang of those days was known as a 'raspberry' and might even insist on his recall.

The padre deserves an extra mention, for he not only opened a church and a cemetery but also started a school, mostly for the children of the garrison: but when the principal chiefs asked if their sons could come along and learn the white man's magic he did not discourage them. Indeed the Governor himself brushed up his Latin once a year and took part in the examination.

For the most part, though, the Governor was interested in roads; for this is a characteristic which the British share with the ancient Romans. There was, too, some reason for his interest. A Commander-in-Chief who commands two companies is twice blest if by means of a road he can get his blow in first. Besides, he could get more revenue if the produce of the country could be brought down to the coast and sold. The producer would benefit, the trader would benefit, and the Governor would get more taxes to build more roads, which would bring in more produce and more taxes, and so *ad infinitum*. He did not know that by building roads he was laying the foundation of a self-governing Arcadia: but in fact he did; for the highly organised community which the nationalist politicians are now taking over depends upon an excellent system of communications by road, rail and air which enables Arcadia to conduct a large overseas trade.

By his instructions the Governor was advised to create a Council of officials whom he could consult and in whose name his Proclamations or Regulations should be issued. This would ensure more formality in the enactment of legislation, so that everybody would know when the Governor was giving an order and when he was making law. Also, though the local tribunals dealt with ordinary day-to-day problems, it was necessary to establish a Court for the trial of serious offences and to deal with disputes outside the scope of native law, such as those relating to commercial contracts made by the traders who were establishing themselves in increasing numbers. A lawyer was brought out from England to act as Judge, the Governor himself acting as Court of Appeal. Very soon, however, the work became heavy, and so a second lawyer was brought out to act as Chief Justice. A Supreme Court was established and all the complications of English legal procedure introduced.

After twenty years or so the capital of Arcadia was a flourishing city. The country had been divided into provinces and there was in each of them a small provincial capital. The judges of the Supreme Court went round on circuit. The padre's school had grown and multiplied. The pupils were becoming clerks, teachers and interpreters, medical assistants, and even lawyers. The chiefs' sons had become chiefs, but they preferred to live in the capital city and live the sort of life for which their education had fitted them. There was a real public opinion, and the more prominent leaders were frequently consulted. It was decided to formalise these arrangements and to establish a Legislative Council, consisting mainly of officials, who were now much more numerous, but including also some of the local leaders. These were carefully selected so that the various tribes were properly represented and a cross-section of opinion obtained. Objectionable people who might become a nuisance were of course excluded, but they were very few, because the idea of antagonism between officials and unofficials, as they were called, had not yet developed. As a matter of fact, criticism of the Governor came not from the local people but from the European lawyers, traders, journalists, etc., who had been attracted to Arcadia by its prosperity.

There were of course variations in this prosperity. Sometimes prices were high and sometimes they were low. If they were low the Governor was subjected to a great deal of criticism. He was spending too much on roads, railways, hospitals and schools. The salaries of officials were too high. Taxation was too heavy. When prices rose again everybody who mattered was too busy making money to be very critical; but if there was criticism it was due to the reluctance of the Governor to build roads, railways, hospitals and schools. There were not enough schools and teachers to provide for everybody who wanted education. There was unemployment among the educated, because the Governor was not expanding services rapidly enough. It was alleged that he was reluctant to impose taxes on the traders, who were making all the money, because they were Europeans and Indians—the Indians had begun to arrive as soon as there was prospect of profit; for Indians (oddly enough) like to make money. Above all, the Legislative Council was entirely unrepresentative because the Governor appointed his toadies instead of letting the people of Arcadia choose their own representatives.

This problem was met by increasing the size of the Legislative Council. Members elected on a narrow franchise were added, but so were a few officials, with the result that there was still a Government majority of one. Later it was argued that a Government majority of one was as autocratic as Government by Governor alone, because the officials voted as they were told. The argument was untrue. Very rarely did the Governor use his official majority: it was his aim to work with the unofficial members, who therefore had very considerable influence on policy. It was only in exceptional circumstances, when the Governor thought the unofficial members factious, misguided or corrupt, that the official members overrode the unofficial members.

Nevertheless, the rapid social and economic development of Arcadia compelled more and more rapid changes. The population was increasing rapidly both in number and in wealth. A good health service was wiping out epidemic diseases. A good maternity service brought down the infant mortality rate. The development of trade enabled this increased population to be fed and clothed. In particular, it created a large educated middle class in the towns whose members had studied English literature and the British Constitution in the schools. Some of them had even gone to universities in the United Kingdom. Accepting the ideas of freedom, justice and equality which they found in English history, they asked for freedom, justice and equality in Arcadia. They saw no reason why a Governor appointed by the Secretary of State for the Colonies should rule the country, why all the senior posts in Arcadia should be filled by Englishmen and Scots, and why trade and commerce should be in the hands of

Europeans and Indians. The leaders of this nationalist movement were the unofficial members of the Legislative Council. They organised themselves into a Nationalist Party which became severely critical of Government measures. Especially critical were they of their own subordinate position.

This development was met by increasing the number of elected members. This time there was no corresponding increase in the number of official members, and so the unofficial members had a majority. For a short period the nominated members held the balance between the official members and the elected members. But the rapid expansion of English education throughout Arcadia led to quite reasonable demands for an extension of the system of representation by election; and the present constitutional system in Arcadia is what is called 'representative government': that is, the elected members of the Legislative Council are more than half the total number of members. The elected members dominate the Legislative Council. There are still nominated members, because there are still backward sections of the population, organised in the traditional tribal system, which cannot adequately be represented by elected members. There are still official members, because the Governor is still responsible for the government of Arcadia. He has two or three unofficial members on his Executive Council, and they take part with him in decisions on policy; but they are not members of the Legislative Council and they are not in any sense Ministers responsible to that Council. They are simply a means by which the Governor keeps his executive government in touch with public opinion.

It will be seen that what is wanted now is a means by which the gap between representative government and responsible government can be bridged. In previous talks I have discussed the problems which have to be solved in establishing responsible government. In my next and last talk I shall discuss some of the devices which have been used or might be used in the transitional period. For the moment I must explain some of the difficulties of operating representative government.

These difficulties are not new. They arose in the eighteenth century in the American and West Indian colonies. The practice then was to empower the Governor to summon an assembly elected on a narrow franchise which in effect gave control to the wealthier sections of the population. The Governor retained executive authority in his own hands, working with an Executive Council rather like the British Privy Council, consisting of the chief officials and eminent local people. Except in matters of imperial concern, he did his best to govern in accordance with local opinion. It is not impossible for such a system to work. In fact, the old system is still in operation in the Bahamas and Bermuda, in both of which the legislature consists of two houses, a Legislative Council and an Assembly. Until recently Barbados was in the same position. It worked in North America during the eighteenth century because the United Kingdom rarely intervened in the affairs of the colonies. The American War of Independence arose not because of conflicts between the Governors and their Assemblies, but because the Parliament of the United Kingdom tried to force the American colonies to pay for their own defence. The thirteen colonies resisted, won the war, and formed the United States.

The old system continued in Canada—which, as I have explained previously covered what are now Ontario and Quebec—in Nova Scotia and in the West Indies. In Canada there was considerable difficulty both in Lower Canada, or Quebec, and in Upper

Canada, or Ontario. The Durham Report of 1840 suggested responsible government, subject to limitations relating to imperial affairs, as a solution. In this particular case it proved to be no solution, because the communal problem was left unresolved. Lord Durham thought it would be resolved by the English swamping the French. Nothing of the kind happened, and the real solution was found twenty-seven years later, when the Province of Canada was again divided into two Provinces, which were federated with the three Maritime Provinces in the Dominion of Canada.

In the West Indies the old representative system, as it was called, has sometimes worked, but sometimes it has not worked. As I mentioned just now, it was retained in the Bahamas, Bermuda and Barbados, but in the other colonies it disappeared either through local initiative or through Acts of Parliament of the United Kingdom. More recently there has been a second development of representative government through the sort of development which I have illustrated from the history of the mythical colony of Arcadia. It is however even more difficult to work representative government in these colonies because in each of them there is a strong nationalist movement. The older colonies were dominated by European settlers, usually though not invariably of British origin. Their primary loyalty was to the United Kingdom: the Governor was the representative of their King or Queen. They did not always agree with the Governor, but at least there was no conflict of loyalties between the United Kingdom on the one hand and the colony on the other.

In the newer colonies with representative government this is not so. The people of Arcadia feel that they owe a loyalty to Arcadia. Indeed the policy of the Colonial Office is designed to encourage that loyalty.

The people of Arcadia will never be able to govern themselves unless they develop a common patriotism, a patriotism towards Arcadia which transcends their traditional loyalties to race, religion, caste or tribe. We ourselves create the obstruction to representative government because, if we do not, we fail to remove the obstacle to responsible government. There is the dilemma, which I must discuss in my last talk.

There would be less of a dilemma if we could somehow retain in the nationalist movement an element of loyalty to the Commonwealth. When a territory obtains independence it necessarily has the right to secede from the Commonwealth. The Republic of Ireland and Burma, neither of which was a colony, have already seceded. From the point of view of the rest of the Commonwealth, such a secession is unfortunate. Every new nation complicates the international scene. It is less complicated, however, if the new nation remains associated with the collection of friendly nations which we call the Commonwealth. That there are advantages in that association is shown by the fact that India and Pakistan, in spite of the conflicts between the Indian National Congress and the Muslim League, on the one hand, and the British Government of India on the other hand, have decided to remain associated with the Commonwealth as republics, while Ceylon has decided to remain associated not as a republic, but on the same terms as Canada and Australia. Burma left; but it made a defence agreement with the United Kingdom and there are sections of opinion in Burma which consider its action in 1947 to have been precipitate, a consequence of the Japanese occupation. Whether these sections of opinion are right or wrong is not the question. My point is only that we ought to do our utmost to maintain friendly relations between the nationalist movement and British opinion in the difficult transitional period between representative government and responsible government.

What is more, if that friendly feeling exists it may be possible to expedite the grant of responsible government. So long as Arcadia is a colony, the United Kingdom owes a responsibility to all sections of its people. If the Colonial Office considers that there is a possibility of anarchy, or communal strife, or economic disturbance or intervention by a foreign Power, whether directly or indirectly through a party organisation, or a *coup d'état*, it must clearly retain control. If on the other hand it is assured that the new Government is likely to seek such advice and assistance as a friendly Government can properly receive without any loss of sovereignty, there is very little risk in granting responsible government forthwith. In this respect a memorandum submitted to the Colonial Office by Mr D. S. Senanayake, afterwards Prime Minister of Ceylon, in 1945 is instructive. The problem of defence was then dominant because the war with Japan had not ended, and the Japanese were in occupation of Burma and Malaya.

The memorandum pointed out that there were two ways of dealing with the problem of defence, in which both the United Kingdom and Ceylon were concerned—and indeed India, Australia and New Zealand also, for an enemy based on Ceylon could dominate the sea and air routes to those countries. One was that chosen by the United Kingdom in 1943, to give Ceylon control over internal affairs and to give the United Kingdom control over external affairs and defence. That method, the Ministers suggested, could not be effective without the willing collaboration of the two Governments. Defence could not be effective unless there was some control over roads, railways, telecommunications, the use of property, public works, labour, trade and commerce, and in fact a very large part of the field of internal administration: but could it be assumed that a Ceylon Government which had no responsibility for defence but wanted independence would collaborate in this way? The other way was to confer independence and to rely on the collaboration of a friendly Ceylon. In this case collaboration was much more likely because it was to Ceylon's own interest to be adequately defended: and it was suggested that agreements for this purpose might be made at the time of granting independence. The proposal was not accepted in 1945; and in 1947, when the defeat of the Japanese had made the problem of defence less apparent, the Ceylonese Ministers were not prepared to offer such favourable terms. Nevertheless agreements were signed. Ceylon became an independent member of the Commonwealth, and a friendly one, in 1948.

The case will never recur in that form, but the question whether a country can defend itself is one of the questions to be answered, not only by the local politicians but also by the United Kingdom, when the question of expediting the grant of independence is under discussion. Nor, indeed, is it the only problem. External affairs—on which Ceylon also has an agreement—and even economic affairs, may be dealt with in the same manner. One of the advantages of membership of the Commonwealth is that standing arrangements can be made for this purpose. In the realm of external affairs, for instance, the United Kingdom is prepared, if and so long as it is asked to do so, to allow its diplomatic representatives to act on behalf of any member of the Commonwealth which does not wish to be separately represented because its relations with the country concerned are few and casual. In the realm of economics arrangements for technical assistance like the Colombo Plan are possible, though collaboration is often more fruitful at lower levels, where expert consults expert.

The problem is, therefore, how to maintain friendly relations in the difficult period of representative government, while the nationalist politicians spend so much of their time in 'blaming the British' for everything from the excessive consumption of toddy to the insufficiency of irrigation schemes or (and possibly 'and') the inadequacy of flood protection. There are many reasons for the difference beween the villager squatting in front of his mud-and-wattle hut and the European official driving his car into his compound; but the easiest way of explaining it, and the one which gains most votes, is that the colonial power has failed to build the new Jerusalem which politicians all over the world promise to erect as soon as they get into power. When the British voter hears this sort of story on television, he grins, because he has heard it before; the villager who hears it under the mango tree may believe it. This is a danger not only immediately but also at a later stage, when the politicians have come to power; for the new Jerusalem takes a long time to build, especially when (as is usually the case) the supply both of building materials and of money to buy them is very limited. Villagers have been heard to remark that they were better off under the British, though the truth probably is that they are neither richer nor poorer, neither happier nor sadder; for Jerusalem was not built in a day, nor even in the lifetime of any particular political patriarch.

There is of course no real solution to this difficulty. It can be minimised by the exercise of a good deal of tact by everybody from the Secretary of State to the cadet. The clear mandate which the British electors have given their representatives since 1945 is a great help. The unfortunate way in which affairs were handled in India in the 'thirties was, in some measure, the consequence of divided counsel in Whitehall and Westminster, and something of this tradition persisted into the early 'forties. After 1945 there was a definite policy not only of conferring self-government, but of expediting it as much as possible, with the result that the imported officials and the local politicians have had the same policy even if (as indeed always happens) there are differences of opinion about the method and the speed.

Also, the speed of air transport now makes it possible for the Secretary of State and his principal advisers to make frequent visits to the colonial territories where, if they do no more, they learn that their Office is dealing with real people who are, usually, far more sensitive to lack of tact than the Minister's own constituents. Nor is there any hesitation in spending public funds on sending local leaders to Whitehall. When Mr D. S. Senanayake, Leader of the State Council in Ceylon, went to England in 1945, he met a Secretary of State for the first time, though he had been in politics since 1916 and in office as Minister since 1931. Most of the officials knew about him only on paper, and he was a complete surprise to them, for they had apparently expected not a bluff and almost inarticulate old farmer but a ranting politician. This visit was paid at his request and at his own expense (and it cost him £100 a day). Visits of this kind were rare before 1947; now they are frequent. The more the politicians and the officials in Whitehall appreciate the point of view of the local politicians and the more the local politicians understand the objectives and the methods of Her Majesty's Government, the smaller will be the area of controversy. This does not imply that controversy will be avoided, but only that it will be kept to a minimum. A politician in power, whether in the

United Kingdom or elsewhere, has to believe, or at least to claim, that his own administration is admirable. A politician out of power has to believe, or at least to claim, that everybody would be happier if he were in power. A Colonial Secretary, and indeed the whole Colonial Office, is not exempt from the tendency to regard the administration as wholly satisfactory; nor are local politicians exempt from the tendency to allege that there would be vast improvements if it were not for the restraints of the Colonial Office and the Governor. Moreover, the local politicians have behind them the strong emotions of a nationalist movement. They will not admit that self-government may be worse than colonial government so far as the happiness and the standard of living of the villager is concerned; but even if they did they would answer that 'good government is not a substitute for self-government'. The process of 'blaming the British' must be regarded as a normal part of the process of government.

Indeed, it goes on long after independence has been achieved. As this talk was being revised, the press reported that a Commission on Prohibition in India had decided that the social habits of the English had led to the spread of drinking in India. Since most of the drinking in India took place in the villages, where the toddy was allowed to ferment in the chatties or converted into a brew called arrack by distillation, I wondered how this development had been assisted by the few drinks which I had consumed (in happier days, when there was a bar) in the lobby of the Connemara Hotel in Madras. I consoled myself with the reflection that this was simply carrying on the tradition of 'blaming the British'. If it be assumed that the villager will be happier if he does not drink toddy, it must be the fault of the British that he likes to drink toddy, for nobody would do anything to make himself less happy if he were properly governed. Nor is this tendency limited to India. A few weeks ago it was pointed out in the Constituent Assembly of Pakistan that the 'provincialism' which induced the Sindhis, the Punjabis and the Pathans, so it was said, to compete with each other instead of working together as Pakistanis, was due to the British tradition of 'divide and rule'. The British had established the Provinces of Sind, the Punjab and the North-West Frontier not because the Sindhis, the Punjabis and the Pathans wanted to be governed locally and not from New Delhi, nor because it was thought that the Sindhis, the Punjabis and the Pathans might want local self-government, but because the British did not want the Pakistanis (who as Pakistanis did not exist until British rule ended) to govern Pakistan.

These are curious examples of a general tendency which must be regarded as normal. When Ceylon obtained independence in 1947 I remarked in a local newspaper that it would be unfortunate if the tradition of 'blaming the British' were succeeded by a tradition of blaming the politicians, because it would make the problem of government difficult. My fears were groundless. The politicians in power still 'blame the British' when something goes wrong or when they want to make some change that the British did not make; the politicians in opposition, on the other hand, blame the politicians for following the example of the British, or not following the example of the British, as the case may be. Both sides therefore have a perfect stalking-horse. On the other hand, nobody takes all this very seriously. The real problem is to minimise the serious antagonism which does grow up in the period of partial self-government if the manner or the pace of development becomes the subject of controversy.

The answer to this problem depends upon the nature of the controversy and the persons who take part in it. It is possible, however, to make two general observations. In the first place, it is desirable to strengthen the sympathetic ties between the country concerned and the United Kingdom as the political ties are weakened. Something is already being done. The Queen and other members of the Royal Family pay frequent visits to her dependent territories as well as to her independent realms. These visits have an immediate psychological effect, though that effect seems to wear off rather quickly. Nor can one expect such visits to be frequent. Visits by the Secretary of State for the Colonies and other members of the Government may sometimes be even more valuable; for royal visits are necessarily occasions for pomp and ceremony, while ministerial visits involve active consideration of the territory's political problems. A 'high-powered' delegation, such as that which recently visited Malta, is particularly impressive because it shows that the political problems of the territory are not regarded as matters of minor concern, even in a world dominated by conflicts among the great powers. Such visits need to be preceded or followed by detailed investigations, for decisions cannot be taken on the spur of the moment. Even so, it is plain that the recent visit of the Secretary of State to Singapore and Malaya did succeed in removing some of the elements of distrust which are almost inevitable in the conditions in which those territories now find themselves. It would be useful, too, if public opinion in the United Kingdom could be induced to take a more active interest in the affairs of the dependent territories. It may be doubted, however, whether this is practicable. Visitors from every country, not excluding the United States, complain of the little attention that is given to their affairs in the

British newspapers; and the reply that most of those newspapers pay little attention to the more serious affairs of the United Kingdom, though correct, is not satisfying. It is indeed impossible to follow, in the columns even of the serious newspapers, the affairs of countries as important as Pakistan or Ceylon, and even less attention is paid to countries of less relative importance. Probably a better line of development is to make closer the relation between the Crown and its representative, perhaps by appointing a different type of person to the office of Governor. It would be hard on the colonial service to take away the 'plums' of that service, to which the ablest of its members hope to be promoted: but it is difficult, if not impossi ble,for a person who has been promoted through its ranks to secure recognition as the representative of the Queen, the person who bears witness to the personal interest which the Queen undoubtedly takes in the affairs of the territory. He is more likely to be regarded as the instrument of 'imperialism' or 'colonialism', the person who continues to exercise control over the nationalist movement in the name of the Government of the United Kingdom. He is only an official because he is a promoted official. Even the Viceroy of India was regarded as an instrument of 'imperialism', though in fact he rarely had official experience and the office was regarded as one of the highest in the service of the Crown. The King-Emperor was not the symbol of free association but the symbol of British rule. It is not surprising, therefore, that India and Pakistan decided to become republics and that during the recent litigation in Pakistan the existence of any powers in the hands of the Queen or her representative was thought by many to indicate a diminution of Pakistan's independence. As the examples show, this problem is incapable of solution; but in a colony a deliberate attempt can be made to strengthen the bonds with the Crown and to undermine the belief that the Governor is Britain's watch-dog.

My second suggestion is that continued efforts must be made to prevent the exhibition of racial prejudice. This is not a matter which can effectively be regulated by law, as indeed India has shown in respect of the similar problem of caste prejudice. Discrimination on account of caste is forbidden by the Indian Constitution, and some of the States have detailed legislation to give effect to this principle. It is, however, plain not only from observation but from the speeches of Indian leaders and the reports of official committees that it continues to exist. Deep-seated prejudices of this character cannot be removed by legislation, and the best that one can do is to remove the more obvious public manifestations, such as those which are officially maintained and supported in the Union of South Africa. The pressure of opinion is in the long run much more effective, especially when it becomes necessary for the Europeans to work with their 'opposite numbers' among the Africans or Asians. There have been few public exhibitions in India, Pakistan and Ceylon since 1947, because those Europeans who remain in those countries have either to get on with the Asian officials, business men, professional men, and so forth, or get out. What is needed is to project this attitude—or, better still, a genuinely friendly attitude—into the period which precedes independence. Her Majesty's Government have made it plain on many occasions that any type of racial discrimination is contrary to official policy, and it is rarely alleged that officials take part in it. Planters and business men, however, tend to live their own lives segregated from the sorts of Africans and Asians whom they can meet on equal terms. It is on them that the pressure of public opinion is necessary.

XII

THE TRANSITION

IN my last talk I explained the dilemma of representative government. To develop the conditions required for responsible government it is necessary to have a strong nationalist party which puts national patriotism before sectional loyalties. That strong nationalist party is almost inevitably critical of the Governor and his policy. On the other hand, the Governor can get nothing done without the support of the nationalist party because he depends on the legislature for finance and legislation. It is true that he usually holds reserve powers which enable him to overcome a deadlock; but every time he exercises those powers he calls forth further criticism and creates further antagonism between himself and the unofficial majority.

It must not be thought that the Governor is always wrong. The responsibility for efficient government rests upon him and his advisers. The unofficial majority does not want representative government to work well because its aim is responsible government. It is in the position of a parliamentary majority which cannot, so long as mere representative government operates, be called upon to assume responsibility. It is a permanent Opposition which holds the majority but can never be called upon to form a Government and make good its promises. It is therefore not surprising that the majority is sometimes factious and that efficient government becomes difficult. Lord Durham said that opposition between Government and the Legislature was almost inevitable; and the experience of a century has not proved him to be wrong.

On the other hand, full responsible Government cannot be conferred until all the problems which I have discussed in these talks have been reasonably settled. I hope I have made it plain that perfect solutions of those problems cannot be expected. Various constitutional devices, some of which I have mentioned, can be invented to minimize the risks; but some risks must be taken. Even so, there must be a transition. The electors have to get used to the exercise of the franchise; communal claims may have to be sorted out and incorporated in the larger patriotism; a public service, staffed mainly by local people, has to be developed; the parliamentary majority has to learn to accept leadership; persons capable of functioning as Ministers have to be discovered and encouraged.

The question we must ask ourselves, therefore, is how that transition can be eased. I cannot answer the question, because the solution depends upon local conditions. I can do no more than discuss some of the solutions which have been attempted.

First, let me point out that responsible government may be limited in its scope. When Lord Durham recommended what we should now call responsible government he did not contemplate that it should cover the whole field of government. He expressly excluded such matters as defence and external relations, foreign trade, the disposal of Crown lands, and constitutional changes. These, he thought, were matters for the United Kingdom. We know that in fact Canada and Australia gradually encroached on what we would now call the reserved subjects; but that is irrelevant because we now regard this position of quasi-responsible government as merely a stage on the road to complete independence. Nor have I mentioned all the subjects that might be reserved. For instance, in some circumstances, it might be necessary to reserve control over immigration or the public service. In Southern Rhodesia under the Constitution of 1923 the subject of native affairs was reserved.

It is not very easy to divide up the subjects of government in this way, but it can be done. It is done in every federal constitution; and in the United Kingdom we have a division of power between the Parliament of the United Kingdom and the Parliament of Northern Ireland. The problem of definition arises. In 1946 there were long arguments in Ceylon about 'defence' and 'external affairs'. In wartime, defence encroaches upon almost all fields of government, while external affairs might be held to include all forms of economic regulation, such as tariffs, exchange control, immigration, etc. Hitherto it has been assumed that in case of conflict the decision will rest with the United Kingdom, or be settled by agreement. That is not necessarily so. In a federal constitution such disputes are settled by the Courts.

It is nevertheless true that this apparently simple method of limiting self-government temporarily does become rather complicated in its operation. It is therefore sometimes preferred not to try to divide up the fields of government but to give specific powers to the Governor or the Secretary of State or the Queen in Council. There are several ways of doing this. In the first place, a Bill passed by the legislature does not become law until the Governor assents to it in the Queen's name. In the United Kingdom the Queen's assent is a picturesque formality, and in an independent country of the Commonwealth overseas it is a formality. In a colony it is a reality. Hence in the transitional period it is possible to make the royal assent a reality either over the whole field of government or in relation to specified sections of that field. What is usually done, however, is to require the Governor to reserve for the Queen's assent any bill which falls within one of specified categories. This means that the Colonial Office, on a report from the Governor, considers whether the bill is desirable or not, and advises the Queen accordingly. This is not necessarily an instrument of control. It may be used to advise and assist the colonial Government. For instance, when the semi-responsible Government of Ceylon decided to establish an indigenous Bank of Ceylon, the United Kingdom Government consulted the Bank of England, which suggested a series of amendments designed to improve the Bill. These amendments were accepted by the Ceylon legislature, which passed an amending Bill. The original Bill and the amending Bill both received the royal assent.

There is in theory a second method of legislative control. The older Constitutions authorised the Queen in Council to disallow a colonial law within 12 months or two years. It is not an effective method because the law has to be invalidated after it has taken effect, and it is very difficult to work out the consequences. I believe there is no recent example of the use of this power; and it has been dropped from the more modern Constitutions. The Queen in Council, or the Queen by Letters Patent, almost invariably reserves a power of legislation for the colony, even at the stage of representative or semi-responsible government: and therefore, if a colonial law is really obnoxious it can be revoked by legislation from Whitehall.

These are in any case negative methods, and they do not enable the Governor to take positive action. This can be done only by giving him power to act without the sanction of the Legislative Council. The extreme case is that in which the system of representative government becomes unworkable through the opposition or non-co-operation of the elected members. For instance, those members may bring the process of government to a standstill simply by refusing to vote the Budget. In fact, though, this problem usually arises not where the system of government is merely representative, but where there is a measure of responsible government. The system may break down because it is impossible to find suitable Ministers, or because communal tension becomes acute, or because rioting breaks out, or because a political party pledged to sabotage takes office, or even because the territory has involved itself in serious finacial difficulties. The only solution is to suspend the Constitution and to institute what in Asia is called 'Governor's rule'. In other words, a step back to autocratic government has to be taken in order that a step forward may be taken at a more propitious moment. This has happened in the past in such territories as Jamaica, Malta, Newfoundland and British Guiana. There are similar powers in India and Pakistan: the President of India has recently suspended the Constitution of Andhra and the Governor-General of Pakistan has recently exercised such a power by suspending the Constitution of East Bengal.

Usually extreme measures of this kind are not needed; but there may be matters of less importance in respect of which the Governor may have to intervene. For instance, the salaries, allowances and leave conditions of public servants are frequently matters of disagreement between the Governor and the Legislative Council. Imported officials are necessarily expensive because they have to be induced to leave the United Kingdom to work in less attractive climatic and social conditions and because many of them have family responsibilities in the United Kingdom. Their emoluments are a heavy charge on the revenues of the colony and diminish the sums available for the social services. Also, the elected members will be anxious to replace these imported officials by local officials as soon as possible, and there may be dispute whether suitable local officials are yet available. Indeed, it has not been unknown for local candidates to canvass the local politicians in the hope of getting lucrative jobs for themselves. It cannot be assumed, unfortunately, that all local politicians are high-minded patriots, whatever the country may be: and in a colony which has had no experience of responsible government or in which nepotism is almost a virtue, there may be as much log-rolling or even corruption as in the worst type of municipal government. There may be other circumstances in which the elected members simply refuse to provide the Governor with the funds or legislative powers needed to enable him to carry out a policy which he deems essential.

To meet such contingencies, the Governor is often empowered to enact legislation and to provide funds in a case of 'paramount importance'. This means that the Governor is expected to use the power rarely and only in extreme cases. Experience suggests that such powers are not often used, because it is the Governor's business to govern in collaboration with the Legislative Council. It is not always his fault if controversy does develop, but he usually goes to the limit of compromise before he exercises his paramount powers. On the other hand, there have been cases in which paramount powers have been used in matters of quite minor importance. In 1945, when the question of retaining paramount powers of limited scope in the Constitution of Ceylon was under discussion, the Ceylonese Ministers asked that, if there had to be such powers, they should be vested in the King in Council and not in the Governor. As they explained afterwards, a sledge-hammer would not be used to crack a nut; but many nuts might get cracked if the Governor was provided with nut-crackers.

These precautionary powers are often necessary, but still they are negative. They do not help the colony to obtain responsible government, but are designed only to make representative government work with reasonable efficiency. If it be accepted that the purpose of representative government is to help towards responsible government, something must be done to enable the local politicians to share in the responsibility. Actually, even under representative government the elected members do learn something about the problems of administration. It is the practice for the Budget to be referred to a Finance Committee consisting of all the unofficial members under the chairmanship of the Colonial Treasurer. The Head of each Department then appears before the Committee to defend his Estimates. The elected members tend to treat him as a hostile witness, for they begin with the assumption that colonial administration is bad *ex hypothesi*. What is more, this arrangement encourages the elected members to take an excessive interest in such matters as appointments, promotions and transfers of staff. Corruption, nepotism or favouritism may well develop if there are local conditions favouring them. There is also a temptation for the elected members to press for benefits for their own constituencies and so to develop the system known in the United States as 'the distribution of the pork barrel'. On the other hand, the Committee has to allow the official to defend his administration, and in particular to explain why a bright proposal is not so bright when the cost and administrative difficulties are examined.

There are various ways of associating the elected members more closely with the administration. One, which I have mentioned already, is to form a Cabinet responsible to the legislature, but to limit the powers both of the legislature and of the Cabinet by excluding certain fields from the orbit of self-government. I mention it again in order to point out that at this late stage of development it is usual to provide a Second Chamber. If this is wholly or mainly a nominated body it can be used as a brake on the First Chamber, which is wholly or mainly an elected body. If the Second Chamber uses its powers, however, it tends to set up a sense of frustration. Representative government gives power without responsibility to the elected members. This sort of quasi-responsible government confers responsibility without power. It is therefore unlikely that this method can be used except in a colony which has already had a Second Chamber under representative government.

A second method is to divide the field of government into two parts, to vest one part in officials responsible to the Governor and the other part in Ministers responsible to the legislature. This was the arrangement in the Indian Provinces under the Constitution of 1935. Most of the functions of government were vested in the Ministers, who formed the Council of Ministers; but the Governor was given certain 'special responsibilities' in respect of which he did not necessarily act on the advice of Ministers. It may be noted that this kind of provision is not necessarily inconsistent with complete self-government. Even in Britain the Queen may sometimes act on her own; and in a plural society it may be desirable to give her representative power to protect minorities or to do other acts, such as the appointment of judges, where strict impartiality free from political pressure is needed. Pakistan at one time proposed to keep a few such powers in the Constitution. Such provisions are limitations on self-government only if the powers are to be exercised under the control of the Government of the United Kingdom. They were so exercised in undivided India, but they are not so exercised in Pakistan.

If there is a division of powers, or 'dyarchy', of this kind, it is possible to associate in the Cabinet or Council of Ministers the officials who handle part of the field of government and the elected members who handle the other part. This was done in Ceylon under the 1931 Constitution. Ceylon was said to have 'seven-tenths self-government' because the field of government was divided into ten parts, three of which were within the jurisdiction of officials and seven within the jurisdiction of Ministers. All ten sat in the Board of Ministers and were collectively responsible to the State Council for finance, though the officials had no votes.

If this was 'seven-tenths self-government' the system established in Jamaica in 1944 might be described as 'half-and-half'. There the Governor presided over the Executive Council, which contained three officials, two nominated members, and five elected members. The elected members were elected by the House of Representatives and might be recalled by a two-thirds majority of that House. Obviously there may be many more versions of this system of dyarchy, and experiments in that direction are being tried in most advanced colonies. Like all constitutional devices, dyarchy will work if the people concerned want it to work. Colonial officials of the new generation know that they are no longer benevolent despots but that they have to be at once officials, diplomats and politicians. When dyarchy is about to be established, it is usually wise to allow European officials to retire on favourable terms. Generally speaking, those who dislike the new arrangements and who seek to retire while they are young enough to find jobs elsewhere are those who would not be very successful under semi-self-government. Their retirement will somewhat weaken the public service, but it will hasten the process of developing a locally-staffed public service. As I have explained in an earlier talk, this must be an objective because it is very difficult to contemplate self-government with a public service which is in large measure imported.

On the other hand, the success of semi-self-government depends less on the officials than on the elected members. Some opposition if not antagonism is to be expected. The officials are expected to hold the Ministers in check, especially in fields like finance, legal administration and the handling of the public service. They would not do their jobs properly if they always agreed with the Ministers. No doubt they must disagree tactfully and seek to persuade rather than to coerce; but there is bound to be friction. Much depends on the attitude of the Ministers. In Ceylon from 1931 to 1947 the Ministers disliked seven-tenths self-government, sought constantly to get it changed, and protested whenever the Governor exercised his special powers. They had a name for the Governor and the three Officers of State; they called them 'the Governor's Government' and they contrasted it with themselves, who were 'the People's Government'. The three Officers of State were sometimes called 'the three policemen'. Nevertheless the Ministers made the system work because they discovered that they could do a great deal for education, health, agriculture, transport, labour and industry. They did not oppose the officials, except on points of real importance; they gradually encroached on their functions. In the result the diarchic Board of Ministers came to look more and more like a Cabinet. In 1947 the transition to complete self-government was effected easily.

The Ceylonese Vice-President of the Board became the Prime Minister, the three officials dropped out, and a Cabinet of fourteen members was formed.

On the other hand, when the Congress Ministers took office in the Indian Provinces in 1937 they did so on the express assumption that they would resign as soon as the Governor exercised his special responsibilities. They ceased to function in 1939 as a protest against India being brought into the war without its consent. It is however unlikely that the system would have worked if there had been no war, because the Governors could not assume that their special responsibilities were a nullity, and at some stage opposition was bound to develop. History as it is written by Englishmen tends to put all the blame for the Indian impasse on the Congress; history as it is written by Indians very definitely puts the blame on what is called 'British imperialism'. I think the final verdict will be that Britain made a great many mistakes, but that worse mistakes were made by the Congress politicians. It follows that pre-partition India does not provide good precedents. The belief fostered by the Congress was that Britain had no intention of permitting self-government; but in the end Britain had to force the Congress and the Muslim League to reach some settlement of the controversy which was holding up self-government. Ceylon supplies a much better precedent for the success of dyarchy as a purely transitional system. It will work, but it demands tact and good faith on both sides.

There are other methods of associating the elected members of the legislature with the process of government. One is the method of appointing committees of the legislature for each major branch of administration. In Ceylon under the 1931 Constitution these committees were placed in charge of administration and were therefore called 'executive committees'. The system worked with some friction, and it could not be described as a great success. It had several defects. First, it encouraged the elected members to take an excessive interest in the details of administration, particularly as they affected their own constituencies. Secondly, the committees had influence in respect of appointments, transfers and promotions. Canvassing became the rule rather than the exception, and cases of corruption were proved. Thirdly, several Government Departments were made responsible to each executive committee. So long as they were responsible to the Colonial Secretary there had been administrative co-ordination; but when the executive committee became responsible there was only political co-ordination, which meant that there was frequently no co-ordination at all. Fourthly, the fact that every question of principle and many questions of detail had to be debated by seven or eight politicians caused lengthy delays in the process of government. In 1941 the Director of Education could not get any decision for two months or more because the Education Committee was debating the Ceylon University Bill. Fifthly, there was lack of co-ordination between executive committees. Finally, the fact that the chairman of each committee was appointed as Minister prevented the development of a common political philosophy.

This last point was the most important. Some of the other difficulties can be overcome by appropriate action. For instance, the Royal Commission on the West Indies in 1939 recommended that the committees should be purely advisory and that questions relating to appointments, transfers and promotions should be excluded from their jurisdiction. The problem of administrative co-ordination can be overcome by fusing the Departments into Ministries, as in Britain: and so on.

What was important, was that it was devised for a plural society in which a party system had not developed. Because there were no parties, it was impossible to have a politically homogeneous Board of Ministers. The result was, however, that there was a heterogeneous Board of Ministers, each Minister playing a lone hand in competition with other Ministers. Hence a party system never developed.

As soon as internal self-government was provided in 1946, however, the various groups got together and formed the United National Party, which won the elections of 1947 and 1952 and is still in power. The other groups are in Opposition and are still distinct, though they often act together. It follows that the Constitution is still weak because it does not provide an alternative Government. Her Majesty's Government functions as in Britain: but Her Majesty's Opposition does not yet exist.

Nevertheless, the lesson is plain. A party system is needed for Cabinet Government; but one way to encourage the development of a party system is to establish Cabinet Government, even if it be partial under a system of dyarchy and even if paramount powers be vested in the Governor. The Committee system of Ceylon did not fail, because it did lead to efficient self-government. Nevertheless, the other methods discussed in this talk seem to be better.

I must end my series of talks by emphasising that the constitutional lawyer can provide suitable machinery once he understands the nature of the problem: but that machinery consists of men and women acting together for a common end. It is sometimes possible to say that the machine is too badly designed to achieve its purpose. More often defects appear because of the deficiencies in the people who form the machine. No machine will work where there is a strong communist party, because the policy of that party is to wreck the machine. But there may be nationalist groups, as in India before 1947, whose objective is to make 'semi-self-government' unworkable in the hope that it will be followed forthwith by full self-government. This process of 'non-violent non-co-operation', as it functioned in India, was closely studied in Ceylon. There the political leaders, though equally anxious for self-government, came to the conclusion that Indian strategy, far from helping towards independence, was one of the factors hindering it—though of course it was realised that the main factor was the conflict between the Congress and the Muslim League. There was some hesitation before 1942, but after Mr D. S. Senanayake became Leader of the State Council in that year the strategy was carefully thought out and put into operation with great tact and skill. The Constitution of 1931 was difficult to operate; if nevertheless it functioned efficiently that very difficulty would be a strong argument for going further as soon as possible. In the process, too, it was easy gradually to encroach upon the sphere of action reserved to His Majesty's Government; the heterogeneous Board of Ministers, with limited powers, could be made to function more like a Cabinet. Conditions were particularly favourable because of the war with Japan. Defence was a matter for the Government of the United Kingdom; but in wartime it is impossible to separate defence from other aspects of civil administration—such as the management of the railways and broadcasting, the acquisition and use of land, public works of all kinds, finance, and so forth. In fact, the armed forces had either to work with the civil administration or take it over. The Commander-in-Chief had the necessary powers to assume responsibility for civil administration, but he could not justify the exercise of those powers so long as he received collaboration from the Ministers. In giving such collaboration, the Ministers emphasised that its continuance was contingent upon steps being taken to meet the demand for a greater degree of self-government; and their strongest supporter was the Commander-in-Chief himself, who soon discovered that he could get what he wanted by direct approach to the Ministers, but that the machine worked with great friction if he tried to use either his own compulsory powers or those of the Governor.

When an offer of an increased measure of self-government, less than the Ministers desired, was made in 1943, Mr Senanayake again decided to break with the Indian tradition. He decided to give the offer the most favourable interpretation possible, to accept it in accordance with that interpretation, and then to press for more. The offer was fairly detailed, but when it was examined it was seen that on many matters of great practical importance it was possible to hold two views, one giving more powers and one giving less. I was instructed so to interpret it that the utmost powers were obtained, to squeeze the lemon to the last drop. Indeed, it seemed to me that the decision of the Board of Ministers squeezed out some drops that were not in the lemon. Again in 1945 Mr Senanayake accepted less than complete independence, secured approval from the State Council, and won a majority in the Parliament established under the Constitution of 1946. When in 1947 he renewed his application for full self-government he had every reason to believe that the application would be granted, as it was.

The interval between the Donoughmore Commission of 1928, which recommended the first transitional Constitution, and the attainment of independence was thus nearly twenty years, or virtually the same period as the interval between the Simon Commission and the Indian Independence Act: but whereas the greater part of that period was one of conflict in India, the Ceylonese Ministers were able to do much for the development of their country. In present conditions the period would be much reduced. What is worthy of emphasis, however, is that the attainment of independence is much easier if the Government of the United Kingdom is satisfied, and can satisfy public opinion, that the transition can be effected smoothly. As experience elsewhere has shown, nationalist politicians find it easier to denounce all transitional measures and to demand independence forthwith than to work a difficult transitional Constitution. The experience of Ceylon suggests that they may be wrong not to make the attempt.

INDEX

For EU product safety concerns, contact us at Calle de José Abascal, 56–1°, 28003 Madrid, Spain or eugpsr@cambridge.org.

www.ingramcontent.com/pod-product-compliance
Lightning Source LLC
LaVergne TN
LVHW090358210926
848480LV00002B/381
9780521241915